IMAGES OF WAR

AIR WAR OVER NORTH AFRICA: USAAF ASCENDANT

RARE PHOTOGRAPHS FROM WARTIME ARCHIVES

Dedicated to Winston G. Ramsey

IMAGES OF WAR
AIR WAR OVER NORTH AFRICA: USAAF ASCENDANT

RARE PHOTOGRAPHS FROM WARTIME ARCHIVES

DAVID MITCHELHILL-GREEN

Pen & Sword
AVIATION

First published in Great Britain in 2019 by
PEN & SWORD AVIATION
An imprint of
Pen & Sword Books Ltd
Yorkshire – Philadelphia

Copyright © David Mitchelhill-Green 2019

ISBN 978 1 47388 179 2

A CIP catalogue record for this book is
available from the British Library.

Printed and bound in the UK by CPI Group (UK) Ltd, Croydon, CR0 4YY

Pen & Sword Books Limited incorporates the imprints of Atlas, Archaeology, Aviation, Discovery, Family History, Fiction, History, Maritime, Military, Military Classics, Politics, Select, Transport, True Crime, Air World, Frontline Publishing, Leo Cooper, Remember When, Seaforth Publishing, The Praetorian Press, Wharncliffe Local History, Wharncliffe Transport, Wharncliffe True Crime and White Owl.

For a complete list of Pen & Sword titles please contact

PEN & SWORD BOOKS LIMITED
47 Church Street, Barnsley, South Yorkshire, S70 2AS, England
E-mail: enquiries@pen-and-sword.co.uk
Website: www.pen-and-sword.co.uk

Or

PEN AND SWORD BOOKS
1950 Lawrence Rd, Havertown, PA 19083, USA
E-mail: Uspen-and-sword@casematepublishers.com
Website: www.penandswordbooks.com

Contents

Acknowledgements

My sincere appreciation is extended to the following individuals and their collective expertise: Bertram Nold, Bob Johnston, Steve Blake, Daniel Setzer, Brad Hagen and Paul Cann. Many thanks also to the enthusiastic staff of Pen & Sword: Roni Wilkinson, Heather Williams, Matt Jones and Barnaby Blacker.

Abbreviations

AAF	(United States) Army Air Forces
BG	Bombardment Group
BS	Bombardment Squadron
FG	Fighter Group
FS	Fighter Squadron
MIA	Missing in Action
MTO	Mediterranean Theatre of Operations
RAF	Royal Air Force
USAAC	United States Army Air Corps
USAAF	United States Army Air Forces
USAMEAF	United States Army Middle East Air Force
WDAF	Western Desert Air Force

The grades of the officers and other ranks mentioned in the book are those which the men held at the time of the events described.

Assigned Strength of USAAF Groups:

1. Heavy bombers:	48 planes (4 squadrons, 12 planes each)
2. Medium bombers:	57 planes (4 squadrons, 13 planes each plus 5 HQ planes)
3. Light bombers:	57 planes (4 squadrons, 13 planes each plus 5 HQ planes)
4. Dive bombers:	57 planes (4 squadrons, 13 planes each plus 5 HQ planes)
5. Fighters:	75 planes (3 squadrons, 25 planes each)
6. Troop carrier:	52 planes (4 squadrons, 13 planes each)

Introduction

Build-up to War

The rise of militarism by Nazi Germany, Fascist Italy and Imperial Japan during the 1930s convinced many senior US political and military leaders that America would again be drawn into a foreign conflict. At the forefront of a new programme to rebuild America's armed forces was President Franklin D. Roosevelt. As the international climate began to progressively worsen, Roosevelt seized upon the military value of air power – both as a weapon and as a powerful symbol of his nation's resolve. On 14 November 1938, in a secret White House meeting, he outlined a programme to establish an Air Corps with a short-term goal of 7,500 combat aircraft and 2,500 trainers. Such an aerial deterrent, he believed, would be a cautionary warning to Adolf Hitler following Nazi Germany's recent expansion – the Austrian *Anschluss* and the annexation of the Sudetenland (an area of the former Czechoslovakia inhabited mainly by Sudeten Germans).

With Western Europe moving closer to war, US planners believed that strategic bombing would hold the chief role in air power. In this capacity the Boeing B-17 was unrivalled as a high-altitude daylight bomber. To avoid the mistake of relying upon too few designs, as in the First World War, the Consolidated Aircraft Company was asked to start work on another prototype bomber, the XB-24 – the future B-24 Liberator. Contracts had already been issued for a new generation of fighter aircraft to replace the Curtiss P-36 Hawk. These designs included the Bell P-39 Airacobra, the Curtiss P-40 Warhawk and the Lockheed P-38 Lightning. Newly available funding allowed the army to order 524 P-40s (in addition to the 200 already on order), thirteen YP-38s and twelve YP-39s (the Y prefix indicating operational testing). It was believed that heavy bomber formations could defend themselves against enemy interceptors, leaving the three pursuit – 'P' – aircraft to operate at low or medium altitudes as well as supporting troops on the ground. To fill the gap between high-altitude heavy bombers and low altitude attack aircraft, the Air Corps also called for the development of two twin-engined medium bombers. Contracts for 183 North American B-25 and 201 Martin B-26 bombers were duly signed despite neither plane having flown.

Hitler played his next card on 1 September 1939 when nearly one and a half million German troops invaded Poland – a gamble that plunged the world again into war. Roosevelt vowed to keep America out of the conflict, though it was clear where his understandings lay. Winning his third term in office in November 1940, Roosevelt broadcast his intention to make

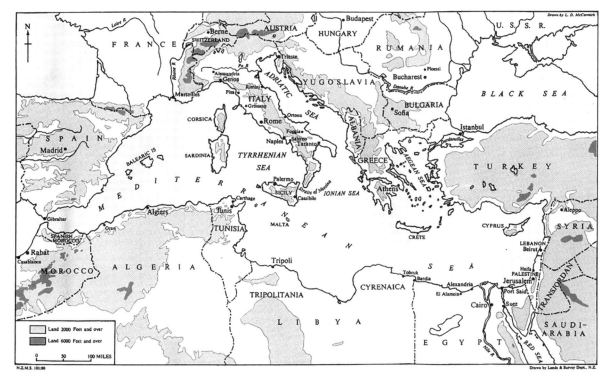

The Mediterranean Theatre.

America the 'great arsenal of democracy'. There could now be little doubt that the world's largest economic and industrial power would soon enter the war on the side of the Allies. Meanwhile the transfer of Luftwaffe formations to the Mediterranean at the end of 1940 was an indication that fighting in this region was likely to intensify. Britain had already defeated Benito Mussolini's advance into Egypt in September 1940. With the withdrawal of Italian forces back into Libya, Britain transferred precious military aid to the Greeks, who had been fighting the Italians since their October invasion. Greece, however, became another embarrassing rout for Rome. Mussolini's series of military misadventures produced an unforeseen new problem for Hitler, who needed to safeguard his interests in the Balkans before invading the Soviet Union. He also needed to 'rescue' his Italian ally, who now requested military assistance. This led to the transfer of a hastily formed German armoured 'blocking force' to Tripoli in Libya in February 1941 and the invasion of Yugoslavia and Greece in April 1941. Despite orders to remain on the defensive, German General Erwin Rommel (the future 'Desert Fox') harried his Italo-German army across the open expanse of the Western Desert – the Nile firmly in his sights. Although he was unable to capture the strategic Libyan coastal fortress of Tobruk, by June 1941 his tanks had reached the Egyptian frontier and the Luftwaffe was in striking distance of the Suez Canal.

US Intervention in North Africa

Since the Middle East theatre was an 'area of British responsibility' at this time, the role of the United States Army Air Corps (USAAC) was initially restricted to providing arms and cooperating with their British counterparts by 'mutual agreement'. American Army Air Corps observers arrived in Cairo in November 1940 to study Royal Air Force operations before crossing the Mediterranean to observe the fighting in Greece. Although the US position at this time was one of neutrality, Roosevelt's 'Lend-Lease' programme supplied Britain with aircraft and armaments, plus the instructors and supervisors needed to assemble, maintain and overhaul US-manufactured aircraft and equipment. Representatives from American aircraft companies also closely monitored the fighting in the Western Desert – a valuable proving ground for their designs. The North African battlefield also yielded valuable insights for US military observers in terms of anti-aircraft defence, supply, communications and the coordination of ground, air and naval forces.

On 21 June 1941, the USAAC was officially placed under a new centralised command known as the United States Army Air Forces (USAAF). It comprised some 6,000 aircraft, 9,078 officers and 143,563 enlisted men. The following day Hitler invaded the Soviet Union. Despite the Wehrmacht's failure to rapidly defeat Joseph Stalin's Red Army, it nevertheless pushed deep into Russian territory. By November the situation appeared critical with Crimea set to fall. Would a German thrust through the Caucasus follow? The danger of a Soviet collapse would have severe ramifications in the Middle East, with a possible German push to seize the substantial oilfields of Iran and Iraq. Coinciding with the Red Army's counterattack around Moscow on 6 December 1941 was a communiqué from Tokyo to the Japanese ambassador in Washington. Decrypted by US Navy intelligence it was, as Roosevelt declared, 'war'. In the wake of the Japanese surprise attack on Pearl Harbor on 7 December 1941, Japanese emissaries delivered a note to Washington cutting diplomatic relations. The US declared war on Japan the next day. Three days later both Germany and Italy declared war on America as allies of Japan. In Washington it was decided that the US would jointly fight the three Axis powers (Germany, Italy and Japan) with a 'Germany-first' strategy.

The year 1942 began badly for the Allies. German U-boats were indiscriminately sinking merchant shipping off America's east coast and in the Caribbean. Allied fortunes were no better in the Far East under the relentless Japanese advance. Britain lost Hong Kong and would soon face defeat in its defence of Singapore; the US was struggling to hold the Philippines; and the Soviet Union was fighting a series of bitter winter offensives against German forces, now halted at the gates of Moscow. Rommel's surprise 1942 offensive brought a renewed threat to Egypt. Britain's Desert Air Force was strengthened with the arrival of US fighters and medium and heavy bombers originally intended for India, Australia, Russia and the Far East. Washington also agreed to commit nine combat groups to North Africa, seven of which would be operational by the end of the year. In the interim, twenty-three B-24D bombers under the command of Colonel Harry A. Halverson were diverted from a stopover in Africa, en-route to the 10th Air Force in China, in June 1942. On the night of 11/12 June, thirteen of these 'HALPRO' bombers took off from an RAF base in Egypt to strike a blow against Hitler's precious fuel supply by bombing the large Romanian oil refinery complex at Ploesti. The raid, which marked the beginning of a concerted American presence in the Mediterranean theatre, was also the first US combat mission against German forces in Europe. It was followed by a joint strike with the RAF against an Italian naval force off Taranto (Italy) on 15 June.

The disastrous fall of the Allied-held fortress at Tobruk on 21 June 1942 prompted Roosevelt to transfer additional arms to the Middle East. Major General Lewis H. Brereton, commander of the US 10th Air Force in India was directed to send as many aircraft as possible to assist British forces now withdrawing into Egypt. Nine decrepit B-17 bombers, described as 'near cripples', were duly dispatched. Brereton arrived in Cairo on 25 June, together with 225 assorted staff officers, pilots and mechanics. While Brereton was taking steps to form the 9th Air Force, three of the nine promised groups for the Middle East arrived: the 57th Fighter Group, equipped with P-40s; the 12th Bombardment Group (Medium), with fifty-seven B-25s; and the 98th Bombardment Group (Heavy) with its thirty-eight B-24s. On 28 June the United States Army Middle East Air Force was activated under Brereton. Two days later its bombers began pounding Rommel's extended supply lines. With the exception of the B-17 and B-24 squadrons, Brereton's aircraft were attached to Britain's Western Desert Air Force (WDAF) under Air Vice Marshal Sir Arthur Coningham. This aggressive New Zealander helped to check Rommel's advance forces at the Egyptian rail halt at El Alamein in July. Bloody fighting continued for the remainder of the month until both sides had fought to a standstill.

On the evening of 23 October 1942, General Bernard L. Montgomery (commander of Britain's Eighth Army) launched an operation that became known as the second battle of Alamein. Preceded by a four-hour artillery barrage, the ensuing battle was mainly fought on the ground with dogged tank and artillery duels. Allied fighters and medium bombers, which hit enemy infantry positions, tanks and supply lines, also maintained a constant patrol over forward Luftwaffe airfields. Although US aircraft played a relatively minor role, P-40s from the 57th Fighter Group shot down twenty-nine enemy aircraft while B-25s helped to break up two enemy counter-attacks. The pivotal battle for Egypt was over by 4 November with Rommel and his Axis troops in full retreat. The newly operational US 9th Air Force harassed beleaguered Axis racing columns across Libya and into eastern Tunisia where Rommel linked up with newly arrived German formations rushed across the Mediterranean. Brereton, at this time, benefited greatly from observing Coningham and Montgomery's close cooperation; indeed it would quickly serve as a model for future US air-ground cooperation. American air power in the meantime continued to grow. By the end of 1942, 370 replacement aircraft had arrived for the 9th Air Force, mainly P-40s, B-24s and B-25s, plus more than fifty C-47 transports.

Operation Torch
Despite the US War Department pushing for a new European front against Germany, Winston Churchill pressed for an invasion of northwest Africa, an undertaking dubbed Gymnast and later renamed Torch. Operation Torch, as agreed, would seize Vichy French North Africa and trap Rommel between US troops to the west and British troops in the east. Planning called for a series of amphibious landings under Major General Dwight D. Eisenhower, involving mostly US troops (for political considerations), which would take place on 8 November on Vichy-held French colonial territory near Casablanca on the Atlantic coast of Morocco, and on the Algerian coast near Algiers and Oran. This would be the first major Allied invasion of the war against the Axis forces and, ultimately, the first major victory for the Allied coalition. Experience

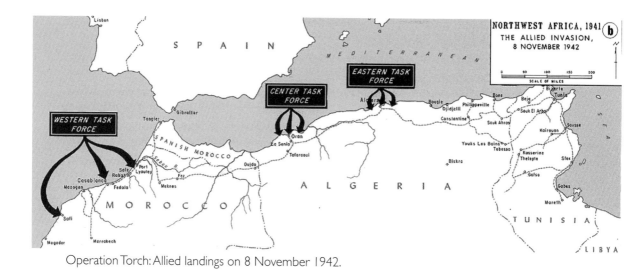

Operation Torch: Allied landings on 8 November 1942.

gained on the battlefield would prove invaluable in the forthcoming Sicilian campaign and the later Allied landings in Normandy in June 1944.

In the early hours of 8 November 1942, three Allied task forces, commanded by Eisenhower, began their first combined assault against Vichy French positions across north-western Africa. The western task force, led by Major General George S. Patton with US troops, landed near Casablanca (in central-western Morocco), initially meeting stiff resistance. To the east, Major General Lloyd Fredendall's US-dominated centre task force approached Oran (in north-west Algeria). After seizing the port, the force moved inland to relieve paratroopers assigned the capture of the vital airfields at La Sénia and Tafaraoui. The Eastern Task Force, which comprised mainly British troops under Major General Charles Ryder, landed at Algiers and seized important Maison Blanche airfield. Ahead lay the capture of Tunisia and its capital, Tunis.

Eisenhower now rushed to occupy Tunisia while the Axis consolidated its strength. The governing Vichy French administration allowed the Axis to operate from its all-weather airfields while the Allies struggled to operate within operational range of eastern Tunisia. US reconnaissance flights noted enemy dive-bombers at El Aouina airfield, in Tunis, and fighters scattered the rest of the country. German Ju 52 transports were also observed at Trapani in Sicily. Realising the urgency of the situation, Eisenhower ordered British and American airborne units to capture the forward Algerian airfields at Bône and Youks-les-Bains, near the Tunisian border. A race had begun to capture Tunis. By the end of November, advancing Allied ground forces under Lieutenant General Kenneth Anderson were just sixteen miles west of the capital. On 28 November 1942 the two sides clashed. Experienced German formations under General Hans-Jürgen von Arnim engaged Eisenhower's largely untested troops, pushing them back some twenty miles to the west. The arrival of winter rains further complicated the Allied situation, turning unpaved airfields and roads into muddy quagmires. On the other side, Luftwaffe pilots flew from modern airfields in Sardinia, Sicily and Tunisia. Amid the worsening weather in December 1942, Eisenhower grudgingly went onto the defensive. This left the bombers and fighters of Major General James H. Doolittle's 12th Air Force, which was activated on 20 August 1942, to continue the fight.

Original plans for Torch detailed the appointment of an overall Allied air commander, though Eisenhower had ruled against a coalition air force. As a consequence, throughout November and December 1942 US and British airmen were engaged in separate battles, primarily in the support of their respective ground forces. This ineffectual situation was resolved at the end of 1942 when Eisenhower and his senior officers consolidated Allied air resources into a single theatre organisation, Mediterranean Air Command, under the command of Air Chief Marshal Arthur Tedder. Tedder was now able to direct air support to where it was needed most. On the ground, Eisenhower's troops faced a renewed test at the end of January 1943 with a new German offensive. This was followed in mid-February by a second German push, this time under Rommel, which defeated the US II Corps at Kasserine Pass. An Allied counterattack several days later, however, reversed German fortunes and helped seal the fate of the Axis in North Africa.

Eisenhower, nevertheless, was critical of the hastily formed and trained US air units then in action. As an example of aerial incompetence he cited a B-17 bombing mission against enemy troops at Kasserine Pass. A complete failure, the bombers, which had navigated by pure reckoning, unloaded their bombs more than 100 miles from target. A reorganisation of Allied air power led to the formation of the Northwest African Air Forces, a component of the Allied Mediterranean Air Command, under of Lieutenant General Carl A. Spaatz. The NAAF, formed on 18 February, comprised the fledgling US 12th Air Force and the WDAF. Rommel's shock victory at Kasserine, coupled with internal squabbling over the management of close air support control, prompted Eisenhower to undertake further reorganisation with the formation of a centralised Allied Air Support Command under Coningham. Allied tactical aviation was immediately transformed with the introduction of Coningham's philosophy to first destroy the Luftwaffe before isolating the battlefield – a combat-proven doctrine used by the British at El Alamein and afterwards in the pursuit of Rommel across the Western Desert. In a presentation to Eisenhower and senior Allied officers on 16 February 1943, Coningham emphasised that the 'Army has one battle to fight, the land battle. The Air [Force] has two. It has first of all to beat the enemy in the air, so that it may go into the land battle against the enemy land forces with the maximum possible hitting power.'

An improvement in the weather in March 1943 permitted the growing number of Allied aircraft to fly, with many operating from newly operational airfields. Under the strategic shift from daylight patrols and close support to air superiority, Spaatz directed Doolittle's strategic bombers against enemy airfields in Italy and Coningham's bombers against Axis airfields across Tunisia. Tactical fighters flew in support of air superiority. By mid-April, the majority of Axis aircraft were either destroyed or evacuated from Tunisia. US Fighters and fighter-bombers could now deliver the support army commanders requested. The *coup de grâce* to the Axis airlift to North Africa was delivered on 18 April. Alerted by Ultra intelligence, forty-six P–40s and eleven RAF Spitfires ambushed a large Luftwaffe air armada off the Tunisian coast. In what became known as the 'Palm Sunday Massacre', twenty-four Ju 52s were sent crashing into the Mediterranean; another thirty-five force-landed in Tunisia. This success, in concert with other attacks in coming weeks, including the destruction of an entire Me 323 convoy, forced the Germans to abandon their daylight supply sorties. On the ground, Allied units in the west linked up with Montgomery's forces driving from the east. The noose was tightening. Axis troops were pushed back to Bizerte and Tunis, their backs to the Mediterranean. Desperate fighting continued throughout April. Allied air power remained dominant. On 6 May alone, Coningham's planes flew more than 2,000 sorties in support of Allied troops entering Tunis. Axis resistance began to crumble and within days some 240,000 enemy troops surrendered, a catastrophe second only in magnitude to the German defeat at Stalingrad.

In Washington it was acknowledged that the US experience in North Africa required a rethinking of existing American air-ground doctrine. A new Field Manual 100-20, *Command and Employment of Air Power*, published on 21 July 1943, dictated that air superiority was the first priority. Second was air interdiction and third was close air support of ground troops. According to the manual: 'Land power and air power are co-equal and interdependent forces; neither is an auxiliary of the other. The gaining of air superiority is the first requirement for the success of any major land operation... Land forces operating without air superiority must take such extensive security measures against hostile air attack that their mobility and ability to defeat the enemy land forces are greatly reduced. Therefore, air forces must be employed primarily against the enemy's air forces until air superiority is obtained... The inherent flexibility of air power is its greatest asset... Control of available air power must be centralised and command must be exercised through the air force commander if this inherent flexibility and ability to deliver a decisive blow are to be fully exploited. Therefore, the command of air and ground forces in a theatre of operations will be vested in the superior commander charged with the actual conduct of operations in the theatre, who will exercise command of the air forces through the air force commander and command of ground forces through the ground force commander.'

US aircraft based in North Africa supported the invasion of enemy-held islands in the Sicilian strait (including Pantelleria) in June 1943, the invasion of Sicily in July, and the landings on the Italian mainland in September. North African airfields were also vital to several strategic bombing missions flown against European targets: B-24 'Heavies' from the 9th Air Force flew from Egypt against the Ploesti oil refineries on 1 August 1943; 8th Air Force B-17s landed in North Africa after bombing the Messerschmitt workshops at Regensburg, Germany, on 17 August 1943. The 15th Air Force, which was established on 1 November 1943, also briefly flew from airfields in Algeria and Tunisia before transferring to Italy on 10 December.

This book is a pictorial account of US fighter aircraft and bombers, the airmen and aircrews that fought to establish ascendancy over North African skies and beyond.

A stick of bombs falling toward the El Aouina Airport, Tunis, Tunisia (top of picture). *Life* magazine, 17 May 1943, reported on the intensity of the bombing campaign against retreating Axis forces: 'The most concentrated air attack of the war', soberly read the 6 May Allied communiqué from Tunisia. 'For nine hours that day four planes a minute went over to smear the German positions. Awed and grateful, infantrymen shook the hand of an airman whenever they could find them. A total of 2,500 sorties were flown that day, following a day of 1,500 sorties. From 8 November to 2 May, the Allied Air Forces in North Africa, including the US 12th and 9th and the RAF, had dropped 9,000 tons of bombs on the Axis, destroyed 1,655 enemy planes against a loss of 631. This was airpower with a vengeance'.

A 9th Air Force convoy stops to 'brew up' and rest a few minutes before continuing on to a landing ground newly captured from retreating Germans and Italians.

B-17 Flying Fortresses pass over Rabat, the capital of Morocco, during a Fourth of July parade, 1943.

Chapter One

Fallen Eagles

Hitler's swift victory over Poland in 1939 concealed a number of weaknesses that would shortly plague the Luftwaffe. Aircraft production was based on the rationale of a short European war, without the need to upscale manufacturing nor radically improve the Luftwaffe's existing types of fighter and bomber aircraft. Production, however, was soon outstripped by the Allies. And a war of attrition would be fought in which the Luftwaffe was beaten in machines and pilots. Unlike Britain or America, the Luftwaffe never had an operational long-range heavy bomber. Instead the Luftwaffe was reliant upon its medium bombers such as the Heinkel He 111 and the Dornier Do 17. The Luftwaffe's doctrine, based partly on experience in the Spanish Civil War, called for aviation to cooperate closely with ground forces. In North Africa, the Luftwaffe was similarly entrusted to provide 'maximum support of army units' and not aerial superiority. German airmen faced long lines of communication, a continual enemy build-up and little prospect of reinforcement.

B-25s of the 9th Air Force pass over the wreckage of a German Me 210 heavy fighter and ground-attack aircraft.

Aerial view of Tripoli during a US bombing raid on Axis shipping and port facilities, 29 November 1942.

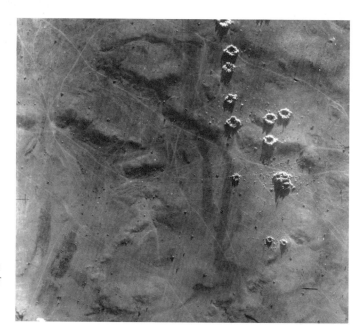

Rommel would later write during his withdrawal from Kasserine in Tunisia that his forces experienced 'hammer-blow air attacks ... of a weight and concentration hardly surpassed by those we suffered, earlier at El Alamein. The attacks ... gave an impressive picture of the strength and striking power of the Allied air force.'

Aerial bombardment of the Axis aerodrome in Tripoli, Tripolitania. Direct hits destroy a hangar (1) near misses explode in an orchard (4) behind the flight line. The two hangars in the upper right were destroyed during previous raids. Personnel quarters and machine shops (2) have been battered. A small lot in the centre (3) is filled with wrecked aircraft.

Dornier Do-24 flying boat CH+ET stripped and abandoned ashore at Mersa Matruh by retreating Axis forces. Note the white Mediterranean theatre fuselage band. The Reich Air Ministry held a preference for the Blomm & Voss BV 138 *Seedrache* (Sea Dragon) flying boat over the Do 24, concluding that 'Dornier should focus on its bombers.' Nevertheless a total of 279 Do-24s were built. Six former Dutch boats were transferred to the Royal Australian Air Force after the fall of the Netherlands East Indies to the Japanese, making it one of the few operational aircraft to have served on both sides during the war.

Junkers Ju 88 wreck, coded 7A+LH, minus souvenired tail swastika.

Derelict Ju 88 fuselages including Ju 88A, coded L1+GT, in the background.

A captured Romanian Ju 88D-1 was flown by B-25 pilots Major W.E Newby and Lieutenant G.W. Cook from Egypt across the Atlantic for evaluation at Wright Field, Ohio, in 1943. Newby described his first evaluation flight before attempting the long journey to America: 'Speeding down the runway I knew that this Ju 88 was the heaviest and most vicious airplane that I had ever flown. It was like trying to get a boxcar into the air. When we reached the proper take-off speed of 160 to 180 kilometres per hour it was still glued to the ground. By this time we had used up three-fourths of the runway and there was nothing we could do but sit there and pray that this hunk of crate would clear herself. Finally, in desperation, I snapped the switch which retracted her wheels and swooshed through the tops of a row of palm trees... At about 4,000 feet we levelled off and had time to check the reason for such a delayed take-off. Much to my astonishment, when I tried to raise the flaps the signals showed they were already in up position. The automatic flaps were too automatic. For an hour we circled the field, and we noticed that the engines were smoking considerably more than we were used to in American planes. But this we considered normal, because in combat we had seen a lot of enemy aircraft trailing this smoke. It didn't worry us. We negotiated a landing, ate a light lunch, refuelled and took off on the first leg of our cross-continent, trans-Atlantic flight. This time the ship got into the air after a short run and from then we began to have more confidence in the plane Hitler had given us.'

Under new ownership. Seen here at Wright Field with US insignia, the Ju 88 was evaluated before being put in storage at Davis Monthan Field in Arizona. Today the aircraft can be seen at the US Air Force Museum at Wright-Patterson Air Force Base in Ohio.

Inspecting a cache of captured Luftwaffe SC 50kg bombs. The Germans classified their high-explosive bombs according to the type of casing and the weight of the bomb. Three main types of high explosive bomb were used: *Sprengbombe-Cylindrisch*, SC, thin-skinned general-purpose bomb; *Sprengbombe-Dickwandig*, SD, thick-cased semi-armour-piercing fragmentation; and *Panzerbombe-Cylindrisch*, armour-piercing bomb, PC.

A US serviceman plays the role of *Waffenmeister*, removing the fuse from a German 500kg SC bomb (fitted with a drum type tail) in a captured bomb dump.

Two bulbous SC 1000 (1,000kg) bombs nicknamed 'Hermann' after the Luftwaffe's Reichsmarschall, are seen here on a *Transportgestell* sled in front of a wrecked He 111-H bomber at Benghazi. Unlike the bombs used by the RAF and USAAF, the tail assemblies of Luftwaffe bombs were permanent fixtures that consisted of four shaped vanes attached to the bomb body by either screws or rivets. Struts or a metal hoop strengthened the tail assembly of bombs weighing more than 250kg. A colour stripe, just visible on the left-hand bomb, denoted the class of bomb; yellow for SC, red for SD and dark blue for PC. Note the British biplane far right.

Burnt out Heinkel He 111 photographed at Benina, Benghazi, Libya.

Heinkel He 111, possibly coded 1H+DF, with white Mediterranean theatre fuselage band at El Aouina. The He 111 is probably the most distinctive German bomber of the war with its leaf-like wing shape and distinctive 'greenhouse' nose. It was the Luftwaffe's third medium bomber, along with the Junkers Ju 88 and the Dornier Do 17. Along with these other pre-war designs, the He 111 served for the duration of the war on all fronts. The Japanese evaluated in-licencing the bomber, which would have received the Imperial Japanese Army designation Type 98, before abandoning the idea. Licence-built examples produced by CASA in Spain and powered by Rolls-Royce Merlin engines remained in service until the 1960s. Just over 6,500 examples were built between 1935 and 1944.

Abandoned twin-engined Messerschmitt Bf 110 D *Zerstörer* (Destroyer). The aircraft was conceived in the 1930s as a multipurpose aircraft that served in long-range escort fighter, ground attack, reconnaissance, fighter-bomber and night-fighter roles. Yet this hoped-for role diversity was a shortcoming that compromised performance compared to more specialised Allied aircraft such as the Lockheed P-38.

This Dornier Do 17 Z was found at Castel Benito, a former *Regia Aeronautica* airfield in southern Tripoli. Regularly seen in newsreels above the pre-war Nuremburg rallies, the Do 17, which was known as the *Fliegender Bleistift* (Flying Pencil) because of its distinctive silhouette, was all but obsolete by the time it entered service in North Africa. Like the Heinkel He 111, the Do 17 was a militarised conversion of a German pre-war civilian aircraft first developed in 1932. Its primary shortcoming was its small bomb load and limited range, which left it eclipsed by the larger bomb load of the Heinkel He III and the superior speed and range of the Junkers Ju 88. Croatian volunteers, the Bulgarian Air Force, the Royal Romanian Air Force and Finland, also flew the Do 17 during the war.

Castel Benito airfield under new ownership. Note the operations tower, roofless hangar, and the burnt-out wreckage of a Focke-Wulf Fw 200 *Condor*. A Condor was the first German aircraft to be shot down by USAAF pilots during the war when a P-40 and P-38 intercepted one off Iceland on 15 August 1942.

German aircraft engines at Benina, Libya. In the foreground is a Junkers Jumo 211, the inverted V-12 engine used in the Junkers Ju 87, Ju 88 and Heinkel He 111H.

Various wrecked Junkers Ju 52/3m transports, the 'm' indicating three engines. According to British test pilot Eric 'Winkle' Brown, the aircraft had the appearance of a 'fantastic amalgam of corrugated skinning, trailing flapper and heavily-braced undercarriage, not to mention a trio of air-cooled radial engines, which, as I was to discover, possessed all the discordance of a phalanx of over-revving lawnmowers [and] demonstrated a total disregard for the most elementary aerodynamic considerations!' The aircraft, however, was loved by German crews and troops who nicknamed it *Tante Ju* (Auntie Ju) or *Eisernes Annie* (Iron Annie).

Junkers Ju 87B or Stuka (from *Sturzkampfflugzeug*, meaning 'dive bomber') captured intact on a desert landing field. First used operationally in the Spanish Civil War in 1936, this infamous, yet obsolete, aircraft was used throughout the fighting in North Africa. Perhaps the aircraft's most significant action in support of Rommel's forces was in the 1941 and 1942 Axis assaults against Tobruk. Large, slow and ungainly with its large fixed undercarriage, the aircraft was easy prey when not protected by German fighters. In one encounter on the morning of 11 November 1942, a squadron of South African P-40s intercepted a sortie of fifteen Ju 87s. Twelve were promptly shot down. The remaining three fell victim to US P-40s later the same day. During the last days of the fighting in Tunisia, Ju 87s were only flown if there was sufficient cloud cover to hide from Allied fighters.

Inspecting Junkers Ju 87-D, S7+EP, El Aouina, Tunisia. November 1942. Abandoned enemy aircraft were often employed to bring up supplies from the rear. The Italians, who lacked dive-bombers, also employed a small number of Ju 87 B-2 aircraft, calling it the *Picchiatello* (or Crazy Diver). The aircraft was also exported to the Bulgarian Air Force and the Royal Romanian Air Force. Nearly 6,500 Ju 87s were built.

A captured Messerschmitt Bf 109G-6 trop (tropical) is examined after it was abandoned in March 1943. It was later reconditioned and repainted by men of the 87th FS in Tunisia. The Bf 109 was the most dangerous adversary of P-40 pilots in North Africa. Nearly 70 per cent of all Bf 109s built were the 'G' models which pilots colloquially named the Gustav. The inverted mounting of the fighter's DB 605 A engine, rated at 1,475 hp, provided superior pilot visibility, a lower centre of gravity and improved maintenance access. (Note the designations Bf 109 and Me 109 were interchanged in Germany during the war. American reports commonly referred to a ME 109.)

German Bf 109 ace Eduard Neumann (thirteen confirmed victories): 'Endless hours of flying, an erratic diet, difficulty in obtaining fresh water, sand fleas, flies, the heat, and also the cold at night made North Africa a very inhospitable place. Mental and physical exhaustion were to be expected in any theatre of the war, and we always had the fear of malaria. This exhaustion happened to every pilot after a period of time … When we heard that American forces had landed in Algeria and Morocco in November [1942], we knew that we were going to lose Africa. The British and Commonwealth air forces outnumbered us greatly. We had probably three hundred operational fighters with all the Luftwaffe units, and they had perhaps a thousand fighters available to them, and this did not include the American aircraft that began flying against us from the west. We were simply overwhelmed, until we were forced into Tunisia, where we spent the last four months of our time in Africa.'

The Focke-Wulf Fw 58 *Weihe* (Kite) was a multi-purpose aircraft used as an ambulance, liaison, light cargo transport and advanced trainer. Note the souvenired swastika and 'scribble' pattern camouflage.

US Senators Ralph O. Brewster and James M. Mead examine the bullet-ridden fuselage of a Ju 88 in Tunisia, 1943. Luftwaffe losses in North Africa from November 1942 to May 1943 alone included 888 fighters, 117 twin-engined fighters, 128 dive-bombers and 371 transports. On the ground Hitler had rushed some of Germany's best troops into an indefensible situation, like Stalingrad, from which there would be no escape. Axis resistance collapsed on 9 May 1943 with over 230,000 Axis soldiers taken prisoner.

German Henschel Hs 129 'Red G' ground attack fighter parked within a revetment constructed from wine casks filled with sand. A total of 841 examples were produced with the majority seeing service in Russia. Note the bent propeller blades and tan 'scribble' camouflage over the basic green paint.

The Henschel Hs 129 was designed exclusively for close air support. Sturdy and heavily armed, the aircraft, however, was underpowered with its French 690-hp Gnome-Rhône 14M 04/05 fourteen cylinder, twin-row radial engines. Coupled with the pilot's restricted field of vision were problems with manoeuvrability and engine reliability. Disappointingly, the Hs 129 was only twenty mph faster than the Ju 87. In North Africa its engines suffered from dust and sand intake and would often seize without warning. Nonetheless, Hs 129s of 4.(Pz)/SchlG 1 claimed twelve British tanks during their first reported action in the Western Desert in November 1942. Note the souvenired tail swastika.

Lieutenants Francis J. Burgess and Harold A. Bollerman pictured in front of Henschel Hs 129 'Red B'.

The twisted fuselage of a Ju 52 transport is inspected. An editor from *Life* magazine in North Africa wrote of a 'junk yard for planes… The outstanding feature of destruction was a sort of parking lot where a hundred or so planes of all sizes made a tangle of wreckage that looked like an old-fashioned junk car jungle outside any US town. We had to go close to identify the scraps as bits of wings or landing gear. Around the field itself the hangars and outbuildings were completely smashed up. A somewhat tattered windsock into which a fairly strong breeze was blowing was noticeable as the only item of equipment still in some sort of working order.'

An assortment of wrecks including Ju 52 9P+HS (right) and Ju 88. The remains of over 250 aircraft were left behind by the retreating German forces at El Aouina aerodrome.

Derelict Junkers Ju 52 and Ju 87 aircraft on the El Aouina airfield at Tunis. A female reporter for *Life* described a January 1943 raid on the airport: 'On the morning of January 22, U.S. intelligence officers at a heavy bombardment base on the fringe of the Algerian desert received word that concentrations of German planes were badly dispersed on El Auina [sic] Airport north of Tunis. For some time reports had indicated that Luftwaffe transports were operating on a fairly regular timetable. At 10.30 every morning, weather permitting, squadrons of troop carriers, bearing Nazi soldiers from Sicily to the Tunisian front, arrived at El Auina airport. At 11 a.m. the empty planes took off and headed for home. Hence on this January morning five weeks ago, a formation of Flying Fortresses was ordered to hit El Auina during this strategic half hour … Miss Bourke-White rode in the lead plane, *Little Bill*, piloted by 26-year-old Major Rudy Flack…able and imperturbable veteran of more than a score of combat missions in the European and African theatres of operations. An hour brought them to a rendezvous point where they met another squadron from a satellite base. Their group now totalled 30 Fortresses. Far above them hovered a protective screen of P-38s… The planes set a course halfway between Tunis and Bizerte to deceive the enemy as to which target they proposed to hit… Then the formation made a 90° turn and sped toward El Auina … *Bombardier*: Bombs away! *Pilot*: Close the bomb bay doors. *Bombardier*: Doors closed. Okay to turn… They banked steeply and Miss Bourke-White looked down on the great smoke plumes rising from the blasted airfield. The squadron then began dipping and weaving to avoid puffs of flak that suddenly appeared in the air around them.'

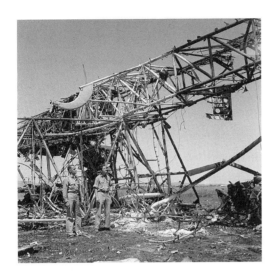

Examining the twisted wreckage of a Messerschmitt Me 323 *Gigant* (Giant) at El Aouina. A powered version of the Me 321 glider, the Me 323 was the largest general purpose aircraft of the war. Note the steel-tube and fabric construction. Powered by six 1,1,40 hp French Gnome et Rhône 14N engines, the Me 323 had a range of 1,100 km and a maximum speed of 270km/h (170 mph), which rendered it particularly vulnerable to Allied fighter aircraft. Fourteen, for example, each laden with fourteen tons of fuel or ammunition, were shot down off Cape Bon during the perilous journey from Sicily on 22 April 1943. A total of 198 of these lumbering giants were produced. The aircraft's designer, Dr Waldemar Voigt, claimed that on one occasion a Me 323 evacuated 220 men from North Africa – eighty within the wings and 140 inside the cargo compartment.

Wrecked Italian Fiat CR.42 *Falco* (Falcon) at Tobruk, Libya. Proposals by Italy – the Luftwaffe's strongest Ally – for the creation of a combined staff headquarters in which some German forces would serve under Italian command in the Mediterranean theatre were rejected outright by Berlin with command arrangements remaining separate. Axis operations in North Africa were further compromised by incompatible radios, the lack of a system for joint control of fighter operations and the Luftwaffe's reluctance to share technology with the Italians.

The Caproni Ca.310 *Libeccio* (south-west wind) was an Italian twin-engined reconnaissance aircraft, which also saw service in the Hungarian Air Force, the Royal Norwegian Air Force and Air Force of Peru. A total of 312 examples were produced.

German General Siegfried Westphal complained that the *Regia Aeronautica* (Italian Air Force) was 'unable to live up to the boasts that Mussolini had made. Nearly all its aircraft were out of date. Even as late as the end of 1941 biplane fighters went into action with a top speed of no more than a hundred and seventy miles per hour.' Mussolini's *Regia Aeronautica* (Royal [Italian] Air Force) was outgunned and out-performed by Allied aircraft – a consequence of the pre-war fascist quest for breaking speed and altitude records in place of developing advanced, operational combat aircraft. Success against inferior opponents in the air over East Africa and Spain had also produced overly-optimistic reports that overrode objective analysis. As a result, of the 3,000 aircraft available to Italy in 1940, only 900 bombers and 270 fighters could be classed as 'modern'. Italy's frontline fighters included the Fiat CR.42, an outclassed biplane, and the equally obsolete open-cockpit Fiat G.50.

A line-up of derelict Caproni
Ca.311s, a versatile twin-engined
light bomber-reconnaissance
aircraft also pressed into service
as ambulance, ground-attack,
transport, trainer and torpedo
bomber.

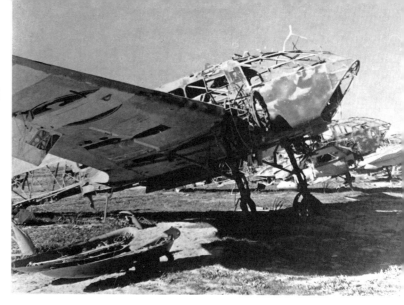

A wrecked Breda Ba. 65 at
Tobruk. Designed as a ground-
attack aircraft, it saw active
service in North Africa and
Iraq. A combination of desert
conditions, poor performance
and superior Allied fighters
doomed the plane with most
lost by the end of 1941.

Two abandoned Breda Ba.88
Lince (Lynx) fighter bombers.
Condemned as the 'worst
operational aircraft' of the war,
many were stripped of useful
equipment and left as decoys
for attacking British aircraft.

Castel Benito airfield and an array of abandoned *Regia Aeronautica* aircraft including a Fiat G.50 *Freccia* (Arrow) in the (foreground), Fiat CR.42 *Falco* (Falcon) fighter (top left), Macchi MC. 200 *Seatta* (Lightning) fighter (top left). Note the B-25 Mitchells landing in the background.

Italian aircraft wrecks inside the bombed-out hangar at Castel Benito aerodrome including a Fiat G.50 *Freccia* (far left) and a Fiat G.55 *Centauro* (right).

Another wreck seen at Castel Benito – a Caproni Ca.111 long-range reconnaissance aircraft and light bomber.

Macchi C.202 *Folgore* (Thunderbolt) fuselages. This Italian thoroughbred was the Regia *Aeronautica*'s finest fighter aircraft of the war.

Fallen eagles at Castel Benito. Note the Heinkel He 111 fuselage in the centre.

Chapter Two

Fighter Aircraft

Curtiss P-40 Warhawk

Curtiss P-40K Warhawk 42-46063 leads a line of aircraft at Gura, Eritrea, a former Italian Caproni assembly plant in December 1942. (For a period Gura was considered a fallback centre in the event that Rommel's Axis forces overran Egypt). Equipped with belly tanks, these newly arrived fighters are ready for action over the Western Desert. The US Army referred to their fighters as 'pursuit' aircraft – designated by 'P' – from 1916 until after the Second World War. The P-40 pilot training manual explained the aircraft's pedigree: 'Since the first P-40 in 1940, there have been fourteen major modifications and many other less sweeping changes in the airplane. The newest P-40, the N model, represents three years of lessons in the hard school of combat. In 1940 the first P-40s were sent to the British. They called it the Tomahawk. By the end of 1940, the B, C and D series were in England. The D was so different from the earlier models that the British gave it a new name – the Kittyhawk. In 1941 came the E model. In 1942 the Allison engine was replaced by a Packard-built Rolls-Royce [Merlin] engine in the P-40F. (This one was called the Warhawk by the British.) Through 1942 and 1943 modifications continued. The Rolls-Royce was replaced by an improved Allison. Better propeller, hydraulic, electric, fuel, oil and coolant systems were installed. The streamlining was improved. The plane was armoured better. Each modification made it a better airplane. The last few models are about as much like the first P-40 as the 1942 Ford V-8 is like the first Ford V-8. Two years ago the latest P-40s would have been the best fighters in the air. Today they've been passed up by newer fighters. But they're still the best, fastest, most nervous airplanes you've ever flown. It requires all of your skill, all of your concentration, all of your alertness, to master the P-40. It is worth the sweat and study. Remember – if you're a good P-40 pilot, you're a good fighter pilot.'

Curtiss P-40 Warhawks of the 66th Fighter Squadron, (FS) 57th Fighter Group (FG), pictured taxiing. Aircraft 41-19984 (left) was shot down by a Bf 109G-6 northwest of Trapani, Sicily, on 10 July 1943. The slogan of the 57th was: 'First in the Blue'.

Late-model P-40F 41-19913 '21'of the 64th FS, 57th FG, 12th AF. Maison Blanche was the name of Algiers' airport during the former French colonial rule. It was so named because it was situated in the suburb Dar el Beida, which was called Maison Blanche because most of its houses were white. Formerly under Vichy control the aerodrome was captured by US troops a few hours after the Allied landings at Algiers on 8 November 1942. In 1978 the airport was renamed Houari Boumediène Airport shortly after the death of Algeria's second president.

P-40Es of the 66th Fighter Squadron, 57th FG. Note the RAF fin flash, which many American aircraft initially carried in the Mediterranean Theatre of Operations (MTO).

Curtiss P-40F Warhawks, 57th FG, October 1942. Note the aircraft numbers split on the fuselage between the US national insignia.

Although the P-40 Tomahawk was initially criticised by the RAF for mechanical difficulties and an inability to operate at high altitude, its performance was nevertheless superior to the British Hurricane. The early unpopularity of the machine stemmed, in part, from the fact that they arrived before US personnel, who were able to provide instructions in maintenance and operation. In the hands of an inexperienced pilot, the P-40 had a tendency to ground-loop and multiple crashes along the African ferry route led to exaggerated rumours about its safety. However, once RAF airmen and crews became familiar with the aircraft, it soon proved its worth in ground attack fighting.

57th FG Easter Service, 1943 at Chekira airfield, Tunisia. This temporary air base was constructed by the US Army Corps of Engineers and used by the 9th Air Force during the Tunisian campaign. To the right is P-40 *Bette III*.

British-made bombs are loaded onto a Curtiss P-40K of the 9th AF's 64th FS, 57th FG. Note the 'Desert Tan' camouflage and scorpion unit badge, which first appeared on aircraft in December 1942, and the painted star on the wheel cover.

Unidentified P-40K of the 64th Fighter Squadron, 57th FG. Although the German Bf 109 was more effective than a P-40 at altitudes above 15,000 feet, the German fighter could not out-turn a competently flown P-40. Lieutenant Mike McCarthy of the 64th FS explained: 'We had to know where they were every moment, to time the "break" call, and turn hard into them so we could bring our guns to bear and shoot.'

Pilots of the 85th *Flying Skull* Squadron, 79th FG, recount combat encounters in which they were individually successful in downing a German fighter. The 79th FG was the second fighter group to join the 9th Air Force.

1st Lieutenant Arthur G. Bury, a member of the 57th FG, warms up his Warhawk before take-off from his base near Burg-El-Arab in North Africa. Seen here is a P-40F (ship #47) assigned to the 64th FS.

Lieutenant Charles W. Tribken Jr. leaves his P-40 after a mission over El Alamein, North Africa. Tribken initially flew in the RAF in a volunteer Eagle Squadron before transferring to the USAAF in January 1943. He returned to the US as a pilot instructor the following month before returning to the European Theatre of Operations in early 1944 and a promotion to captain in the 506th FS, 404 FG. Tragically Tribken was killed in a road accident on 22 November 1944 when a staff car went over a cliff at Toule in France. His death was listed as Died Non-Battle (DNB).

Bob Hope and Frances Langford pose before P-40F *Stud*, flown by Major Robert L. Baseler, the commanding officer of the 325th FG *Checkertails* from July 1943 to March 1944. Baseler was one of four 325th FG aces with six confirmed kills. The travelling USO entertainers were caught in several air raids during their time in North Africa. Recalled Hope: 'Frances and I were standing next to our parked car. We had on helmets. I've never heard such noise. Every once in a while we'd see one of the big German planes burst into flame and come plunging down.'

Lieutenant Robert J. 'Rocky' Byrnes, 64th FS, 57th FG smiles after a successful combat mission. A 9th Air Force intelligence summary from 18 April 1943 records: 'Between 1630 and 1830 hrs. all Wings of the Group were engaged in an intensive effort against enemy transports. Of the four Kittyhawk Wings, three had left the patrol area before a convoy of a hundred plus enemy transports were sighted by 57 Group, who achieved the magnificent score of seventy-four aircraft destroyed. 57 Group were the last in the area and they intercepted an enormous force consisting of some 100 Ju.52s, escorted by large numbers of 109s, 110s and Me 202s. In all they claimed fifty-eight Ju.52s, fourteen Me.109s and two Me. 110s destroyed, and a number of others probably destroyed and damaged. Twenty to forty of the enemy aircraft were seen to land on the beaches around Cape Bon in order to avoid being shot down.'

'The interception of the German transports was no accident', explained General Brereton, Commander, US Army Forces Middle East and Commander Ninth Air Force. 'Intelligence had been observing the air shuttle service across the Mediterranean for some time and they had been waiting for the right time to bounce the slowmoving transports.'

Lieutenant Robert J. 'Rocky' Byrnes, 64th FS, 57th FG pictured in his P-40 after shooting down three Bf 109s on the 18 April 1943 'Goose Shoot'.

The P-40 cockpit was enclosed by a sliding Plexiglas canopy and protected by a bullet-proof windshield. Note the electrical ring-and-dot optical gun sight mounted directly in front of the pilot in addition to the external gun sight.

Major James G. Curl of the 66th FS/57th FG, was awarded the British Distinguished Service Order (DSO) for leading the group on the 18 April 1943 attack – known as the 'Goose Shoot' and 'The Palm Sunday Massacre' – which shot down 76 German aircraft for the loss of only six planes. Curl left the squadron shortly after the mission, later returning to combat in late 1944 as commanding officer of the 2nd FS, 52nd FG, flying P- 51 Mustangs in Italy.

P-40 pilot Captain Roy E. Whittaker of the 9th AF's 57th FG, 65th FS. The highest scoring ace in the Group, Whittaker recounted his part in the Palm Sunday Massacre – the most successful Warhawk mission of the war: 'I attacked the Ju52s from astern at high speed and fired at two planes in the leading formation. The bursts were short, and the only effect I saw was pieces flying off the cabin of the second ship. I pulled away and circled to the right, and then made my second attack. I fired two bursts into two more '52s – again in the leading formation. They both burst into flames. The second flew a little distance and then crashed into the water.'

Before America's entry into the war, representatives from US aircraft manufacturers and personnel from the Army Air Corps provided valuable technical information to the British. With the P-40, for example, the US method of servicing the guns from the bottom of the wing (as opposed to the British method of servicing the Spitfire and Hurricane from the top of the wing) was initially met with disapproval until the benefits were realised. Petroleum sprayed onto the guns from below to clean them would easily drain out through the service holes. Pictured are two armourers working on the guns removed from a P-40F of the 86th FS, the 'Comanches', 79th FG at airfield in Tripolitania, Libya. The P-40F was armed with six .50 calibre machine guns.

A Wrecking Truck Tractor Type C-2, 7.5 ton, 6x6, tows a damaged P-40 for repairs. Note the bent propeller. Pilots were taught that a wheels-up landing requires approximately one-third the landing space of a wheels-down landing.

Tripolitania, Libya. Ground crew prepare to install a Rolls Royce Merlin V-1650-1 engine into a P-40F Warhawk of the 86th FS, 79th FG. Both Packard and Ford produced the 1,080 horsepower Merlin in the US under the Lend-Lease act. The engine's higher altitude rating greatly increased the P-40F's speed at a high ceiling.

Desert conditions took a high toll on engines. In the words of one mechanic, 'We don't use step ladders at all, we stand on large empty gasoline drums while servicing engines. At night we cover up the canopies with mattress covers. If we didn't the glass would reflect the moonlight... Under the wings where the machine guns are concealed are shell extractor chutes. These openings would permit sand to enter and jam the guns if we didn't cover them. So we paste paper from a magazine or newspaper over the chute aperture. With a razor we cut little slits. Then when the guns are shooting, the fired shells can easily force themselves through and out of the way.'

Engine maintenance and an oil change at a 'forward base in North Africa'.

Note the P-40's radiator to regulate engine oil temperature, a system regulated by manually operated shutters.

Breaking open the wooden packing crate containing a factory-fresh P-40K fuselage at Gura, Eritrea. New P-40 pilots in 1943 were instructed: 'You're a fighter pilot now. Your fingers are itching to get at the controls of a P-51 or a P-47. You may be a little disappointed that you have to spend a few weeks flying a P-40. Well, don't be. When you learn to fly the P-40 there won't be a fighter you can't handle. The P-40 is no cinch to fly; it's fast and skittish and responds like lightning to controls. The savvy you pick up in the P-40 is going to make you a good pilot in any fighter. And don't think of the P-40 as a sort of glorified advanced trainer. It's a combat airplane. It's still being flown in China, the Pacific and the Mediterranean – and it's still shooting down Japs and Jerries.'

P-40F 41-19807, 316th FS, 324th FG, following a forced landing at El Saff, Egypt, on 21 February 1943 by pilot Dennis L. Fleak of the 45th Ferrying Squadron, 19th Ferrying Group. The aircraft was subsequently repaired and was being flown by 2nd Lieutenant Donald J. Ellis, 326th FS, 324th FG, when it suffered catastrophic structural failure and crashed on 27 August 1943 at El Aouina.

Refuelling a P-40F of the 86th FS, 79th FG. Pilots were advised how the 'great demands of the overseas air forces have often left domestic AAF stations without a sufficient supply of Grade 100 gasoline. Consequently, Grade 91 gasoline has been widely used at US bases, particularly for training flights. With the tempo of war increasing, Grade 91 fuel will continue to be used. The P-40 is a perfectly safe airplane to fly with Grade 91 gas. With a thorough knowledge of its operating limits, flying with Grade 91 should give you no trouble at all.'

Combat damage to P-40K 'White 11' caused by Bf 109 20-mm cannon shells during combat over Libya on 8 December 1942. Although wounded, Captain George D. 'Muzzable' Mobbs, 64th FS, 57th FG, brought his plane home; 'I took a hit in the left fuselage and took a fragment in my left thigh… I made it back to our landing strip and belly-landed – a very rough belly landing. My trim tabs were ineffective, probably damaged by gunfire, and I was exhausted.'

L to R: 1st Lieutenant Ralph M. Baker, 66th FS, 57th FG; Captain George W. Long, 66th FS, 57th FG, 1st Lieutenant Richard Paulsen pictured at Ben Gardane, 20 March 1943. The latter two were recent recipients of the Distinguished Flying Cross.

Ground crew pictured working on a P-40F assigned to the 86th Fighter Squadron, 79th FG, Tripolitania, Libya. The 79th FG was the second US Fighter Group to reach North Africa.

A-36A 'Apache' & Bristol Beaufighter

One of the new fighter types to see action as the North African campaign ended was the North American A-36 Apache. Flight Officer Dewey L. Gossett's A-36A, 42-83865, 527th Fighter-Bomber Squadron, 86th FBG, bears damage from a 20-mm shell to the right horizontal stabiliser sustained during a dive-bombing mission over Troina, Sicily. Gossett was killed when he crashed in Italy on 27 September 1943. Posted as missing and declared dead a year later, Gossett's remains were finally discovered in a mountainous region in 2014. Posthumously recognised with several awards, including the Purple Heart, Gossett was laid to rest with full military honours seventy-two years after his death at Fort Prince Memorial Gardens in Wellford, South Carolina, on 11 April 2016. Right: Gossett.

The 414th, 415th, 416th and 417th Night Fighter Squadrons received more than 100 'reverse Lend-Lease' Beaufighters, which they operated from Algeria and Tunisia from May 1943. Through the summer they conducted daytime convoy escort and strike missions, but thereafter flew primarily at night. Purpose-built US P-61 Black Widow night fighters began replacing the Beaufighter from late 1944. Pictured beside the aircraft are pilots and radar operators.

Republic P-47 Thunderbolt

Under wraps. Air Service Command (ASC) personnel work to free the guy wires on these newly arrived P-47s. Intended for use as a high altitude interceptor, the P-47's turbo-supercharged Pratt & Whitney R-2800 radial engine provided the aircraft with excellent high altitude performance, a feature lacking in both the P-40 and A-36.

A P-47 is carefully lifted off a barge.

These Thunderbolts, according to the original wartime caption, were 'like elephants in a circus parade … The P-47s are trundled through the streets of the North African port to the airport, while native children and adults enjoy the show.'

A Republic P-47 is received by the 36th Air Depot Group at Maison Blanche, Algeria. The period from September to October 1943 was a transition period for the 325th FG, who were exchanging their P-40s for the new fighter and a period of intensive training. According to the Group history: 'Civilian technicians and test pilots were attached to the group to instruct flyers and to test planes. Lectures, distribution of printed matter, and actual operation of the new planes were the principal methods of instruction.'

An Air Service Command test pilot climbs aboard a Republic P-47 over which ASC's skilled mechanics have laboured for hours, reassembling, removing protective oils and covering, testing and re-tuning.

A Thunderbolt from the 325th FG takes to African skies. The start of the rainy season rendered the field and runway at Mateur in Tunisia unsuitable for operations or training. On 4 November 1943 the Group moved to Soliman, where the transitional phase from the P-40 to P-47 continued in preparation for its transfer to Italy. The 325th flew its first operation mission from Italy on 14 December, escorting B-17s returning from a raid on Athens.

Supermarine Spitfire

Congratulations. 'Two confirmed victories over Jerry in eight days', reads the original photograph caption. Captain Harry L. Barr, 309th FS, was transferred to a newly formed P-39 unit in England. While en route to North Africa his flight encountered bad weather, ran low on fuel, and diverted to Lisbon. Barr was held as a prisoner in Portugal for approximately three months before being released and rejoining the 31st FG in North Africa, flying Spitfires. Barr survived the war and returned to civilian life where he opened a flying school before working in oil and real estate companies. He died on 28 March 2000.

Spifire Mk. Vc (Trop) VF-D, 5th FS, 52nd FG, is stripped for parts after Lieutenant Eugene C Steinbrenner was hit by heavy flak over Tunisia on 9 April 1943. Note the painted-over US flag insignia from Operation Torch and RAF serial number ER120.

Lieutenant R.J. Connor, 31st FG, 309th Fighter Squadron, pictured in his Mk. IX Spitfire with Sergeant William A. Ponder, crew chief. The 31st FG switched from P-39 Airacobras to Spitfires in England prior to the invasion of North Africa. Note the Squadron code WZ. Wrote Lieutenant Norman McDonald, 'If the famous war correspondent Ernie Pyle had not spent a couple of days with us in North Africa, nobody in the States, other than our families, would have known that American Spitfire Groups existed. For about seven months after the invasion of North Africa, our pilots and ground personnel endured living and flying conditions as tough as the worst experienced by any American fighter squadron during the war. We were, literally, the infantry of the air war on many occasions.'

Spitfire Mk. Vb (Trop) EP971 WZ-B, 309th FS, 31st FG, stands on its nose after a landing accident in Algeria, Africa 1943.

Lockheed P-38 Lightning

Lockheed P-38s landing at dusty La Sénia Airfield, Algeria. It was in combat over North Africa that the P-38 earned its reputation. Only the P-38, with its supercharged engines, could match the high altitude performance of the latest German fighters. The P-38 was the first military aircraft Lockheed had designed or constructed. The company's chief test pilot recorded: 'Here was an airplane that was totally new and for 1939 when it first flew was absolutely revolutionary. It had flying characteristics unlike any other airplane up to that time.' Four years later, *Life* (16 August 1943) reported that 'military police brought a dishevelled German flier who was mumbling hysterically and repeating something about '*der gabelschwanz Teufel*'. An interpreter was called, and he had the translation quickly: 'the fork-tailed devil'. Lauding the aircraft, *Life* explained, 'More than winning air battles, the P-38 showed in Africa that it could take Rommel's tanks with deadly effectiveness, strafe with a viciousness unmatched [its guns grouped in its nose instead of spread across its wings, concentrated the fire], come home on one engine and land in Tunisia's mud or on sloping hillsides on its tricycle gear – without nosing over. The Air Forces began to discover as Ben Kelsey, now a colonel, put it, that "this comfortable old cluck would fly like hell, fight like a wasp upstairs and land like a butterfly."' *Life* explained how the aircraft is the 'only single-seater twin-engined fighter plane now used by any Allied air force. Heaviest of U.S. fighters, it is also one of the fastest. It weighs about seven tons (as much as three Cadillac sedans), carries only its pilot, and costs $125,000. Its two engines are worth $16,000 apiece and radio equipment alone, $3,000. Many a pilot has gone through four years of college for less than the cost of a P-38's propellers - $4,000. Its light cannon hammers out nine explosive shells each second and its four .50 cal. machine guns another 72 rounds…it can travel over 400 m.p.h., cruise more than 2,000 miles, climb 4,000 feet a minute. It is so streamlined that 60% of its "drag" is in the landing gear, which folds into the body on take-off. The plane invariably whistles through the air and squeals like a pig in misery before a landing. Despite its speed in flight, it lands at about 80 m.p.h.' From the other side, Luftwaffe pilot Hans Pichler concluded: 'In my estimation, the P-38 was more manoeuvrable and faster than our Bf 109G-6, especially since the latter was equipped with two 2-cm underwing gondola weapons. I had never been keen on dogfights with the P-38, but I did manage to shoot down three of them plus four or five Mitchells. An excellent method of breaking combat was to go into a power dive from high altitude. The P-38 pilots rarely followed us. At first this was unexplainable to us but the mystery cleared up a few months later when a captured P-38 pilot told us their ships became too fast to be pulled out of a dive efficiently.' Over time however, P-38 pilots developed dive-bombing techniques, which they employed frequently.

Lightnings returning from patrol. According to one pilot, 'The P-38 proved its worth as an allround fighter by performing effectively on long-range missions, either providing fighter protection for bombers or putting on a surprise attack on ground forces well behind enemy lines. The only disadvantage, if it can be called that, was the discomfort forced on the pilot by being strapped to his seat for five or six hours at a time.' Wrote General Carl A. Spaatz, 'I'd rather have an airplane that goes like hell and has a few things go wrong with it than one that won't go like hell and has a few things go wrong with it.'

P-38 of the 94th FS, 1st FG, landing after a mission over Sicily. The 1st FG was initially deployed to Britain in mid-1942. After shuttling between UK bases, the group was reassigned to the 12th Air Force in September 1942 to support Operation Torch. After the fall of Axis-held Tunis in May 1943, the group escorted bombers in raids over Sicily and mainland Italy. In the summer of 1944 it supported the invasion of southern France (Operation Dragoon).

P-38G 42-13010 of the 94th FS, 1st FG with pilots (L to R): 2nd Lieutenant Howard A. Gilliam; 1st Lieutenant Leonard P. Stephan; 2nd Lieutenant Harold C. Lentz. Lentz was awarded the DFC on 27 July 1943. His citation reads, 'For extraordinary achievement while participating in aerial flight in the North African Theatre of Operations as a pilot of a P-38 type aircraft. While on a bomber escort mission to Castelvetrano Airdrome, Sicily, on 20 June 1943, Lieutenant Lentz's formation was attacked by 20 ME-109s. Observing 3 ME-109s closing to the rear of his squadron commander, Lieutenant Lentz displayed outstanding skill and daring in destroying the 3 enemy aircraft. On many combat sorties, his gallantry and steadfast devotion to duty reflects great credit upon himself and the Armed Forces of the United States.' Lieutenant Gilliam was killed during the invasion of Sicily.

Algeria. Pilots from the 96th FS, 82nd FG, photographed before Lieutenant J. Wayne Jordan's P-38 *Spud* after claiming 16 aerial victories while escorting bombers over Sardinia. One of their comrades, 2nd Lieutenant George E. Wehman, was listed as MIA flying P-38G 42-12876. Posthumously awarded the DFC, Wehman's citation reads: 'For extraordinary achievement while participating in aerial flight in the North African Theater of Operations as Pilot of a P-38 type aircraft. On 5 April 1943, Lieutenant Wehman's squadron escorted eighteen B-25s on a combination anti-shipping sweep and fighter patrol over the Sicilian Straits. An enemy convoy and a formation of fifty or more Ju 52s, with escorting fighters simultaneously were sighted. Lieutenant Wehman shot down one Ju 52, one Ju 87, conspicuously aided in destroying fifteen other enemy aircraft, and in dispersing the formation. Our bombers were thus enabled to make an uninterrupted bomb run on the convoy, resulting in much damage to the enemy vessels. On his last mission, 18 June 1943, Lieutenant Wehman was reported missing in action after an engagement in which sixteen enemy fighters were destroyed off Sardinia.'

Lieutenant Richard A. Campbell, pilot of the 37th FS 14th FG, poses beside his P-38G *Earthquake McGoon*. Note the one Italian and five German kills. Campbell's first victories were two German Bf 109s shot down on 18 May 1943 while escorting B-17s on a raid against Trapani Milo airfield on Sicily. An Italian MC.202 and a third Bf 109 followed on 15 June and 9 July. Campbell flew in one of the first B-26 raids on Rome ten days later. He became an ace with another Bf 109 on 28 August. In 1945 Campbell served on the China-Burma-India front.

Captain Lloyd K. DeMoss, 49th FS, 14th FG, pictured in front of *Bad Penny*. The 14th FG was the first fighter group to see action in Operation Torch, the invasion of North Africa. Another pilot in the same squadron recalled: 'We had a motto in the 49tth Squadron: "The sooner you start shooting, the better." We always tried to remember that the other fellow has much the same thought in mind, and since we were his idea of a target this motto wasn't to be forgotten.'

July 1943. Group photo of six pilots from the 96th Fighter Squadron, 82nd FG, after the downing of ten enemy aircraft in a fighter sweep over Sicily. L to R: 1st Lieutenant William J. Sloan (12 kills), Flying Officer Frank D. Hurlbut (9 kills), 1st Lieutenant Edward T. Waters (7 kills), 1st Lieutenant Lawrence P. Liebers (7 kills) , 2nd Lieutenant L.D. Jones (3 kills) and 2nd Lieutenant Ward A. Kuentzel (7 kills). In a story filed for the *Los Angeles Times*, Ernie Pyle complimented the job of the P-38 pilots: 'I wish someone would sing a song, and a glorious one, for our fighter pilots. They are the forgotten men of our aerial war. Not until I came up close to the African front did I realise what our fighter pilots have been through and what they are doing…they are the sponge that is absorbing the fury of the Luftwaffe over here. They are taking it and taking it and taking it. And everlasting credit should be theirs… There have been exaggerations in the claims that the Fortresses can take care of themselves without fighter escort. Almost any bomber pilot will tell you that he is deeply grateful for the fighter cover he has in Africa, and that if he had to go without it he would feel like a very naked man on his way to work.'

Corporal Harold Schaffner, armourer from 9th FS, 82nd FG, and pilot 2nd Lieutenant Ward A. Kuentzel, 96th FS, 82 FG. Officially credited with seven kills, Kuentzel returned to the US after the North African campaign as a flight instructor. He deferred further training at West Point and volunteered for combat in China. Sent instead to England, Kuentzel was posted KIA on 19 June 1944 when his aircraft crashed at Petit-Val, Montilly-sur-Noireau, France.

From a different perspective, RAF Group Captain R. W. 'Bobby' Oxspring related his experience in the air with inexperienced P-38s fighter pilots: 'Their aircraft recognition was suspect and in surmounting this deficiency they just assumed that any singletailed fighter was hostile. Anxious to blood themselves, they homed in on friendly and enemy fighters alike, and we spent some anxious moments dodging their headlong attacks.'

P-38G 42-13036, 95th FS, 82nd FG, undergoing repairs. The 82nd Fighter Group flew training missions from bases in Northern Ireland with the Eighth Air Force between October and December 1942. It then joined the Twelfth Air Force in North Africa, supporting the invasions of Tunisia, Sicily and mainland Italy. Between October 1943 and April 1945, the group flew bomber escorts with the Fifteenth Air Force over Italy.

Ammunition is examined before loading into Lockheed P-38G *Babe* of the 14th FG. This group arrived in North Africa in mid-November 1942. Combat losses during Operation Torch were high. By late January 1943, after sixty-nine days of combat, it had lost nineteen pilots killed with another five taken prisoner. Aircraft too were in short supply. Instead of the seventy-five aircraft normally assigned to a fighter group, only twelve war-weary P-38s were operational.

USO entertainer Bob Hope poses with four 48th FS, 14th FG pilots. L to R: 1st Lieutenant George E. Richards, 2nd Lieutenant John C. Meidinger, 2nd Lieutenant A.G. Barber and 2nd Lieutenant Richard E. Jennings. 'Hi ya, fellow tourists,' Hope would greet his countrymen. 'Isn't this a great country, Africa? It's Texas with Arabs.' P-38 43-2543 *2nd Little Karl* #13 was assigned to Major Herbert E. Ross, commanding officer of the 48th FS and a 7-victory ace. The aircraft was named after Ross's infant son. James G. Riley Jr, 49th FS, was flying this aircraft when it was shot down over southern France on January 1944.

P-38F 43-2112 *Sad Sack*, assigned to Captain Ernest K. Osher (far right), commander of the 95th FS, 82nd FG, Berteaux, Algeria, May 1943. From Berteaux, Osher flew fifty-two combat missions, primarily escorting bombers of the 9th Air Force. He remained on active duty until retirement from the Air Force in 1970. His combat record was five aerial kills, four enemy aircraft probably destroyed, and four damaged. Osher died on 26 September 1980.

49th FS Squadron victories: (L to R) 1st Lieutenant Anthony Evans (4 kills), 2nd Lieutenant Wayne Manlove (2 kills), 1st Lieutenant Lloyd K. DeMoss (4 kills), 2nd Lieutenant Marlow J. Leikness (5 kills), 1st Lieutenant Carroll S. Knott (5 kills).

A B-17 gunner in North Africa paid tribute to the P-38 in a poem printed in the US Army newspaper *Stars and Stripes*:

*Sure, we're braver than hell; on
the ground all is swell –
In the air it's a different story.
We sweat out our track through
the fighters and flak;
We're willing to split up the glory.
Well, they wouldn't reject us, so
Heaven protect us
And, until all this shooting abates,
Give us the courage to fight 'em – and one other small item –
An escort of P-38s.*

1st Lieutenant William J. 'Dixie' Sloan, 96th FS, 82nd FG, poses proudly beside P-38F 43-2064 and tally of four kills. Among Sloan's decorations were the Air Force Cross, Distinguished Flying Cross, and twenty air medals. Sloan remained in the Air Force post-war, flying over fifty missions during the Berlin Airlift before retiring as a lieutenant colonel on 30 September 1963. In February 1969 Sloan was awarded the Air Force Cross in lieu of the Distinguished Service Cross he had never received. The citation commends 'extraordinary heroism in military operations against an armed enemy of the United States as pilot of a P-38 aircraft in the North African Theatre of Operations 5 July 1943. On that date, Colonel Sloan led a flight of fighter aircraft escorting thirty-six B-25 bombers in an attack on Gerbini Airdrome. The formation encountered intense antiaircraft fire in the target area and was attacked by ten enemy fighters. Colonel Sloan shot down two of the enemy fighters and was conspicuous in driving the remaining hostile fighters away from the bombers, all of which returned safely. Through his extraordinary heroism, superb airmanship, and aggressiveness in the face of the enemy, Colonel Sloan reflected the highest credit upon himself and the United States Air Force.'

A maintenance crew works on the engines of a P-38 hit by 20-mm shells during a raid over Sicily. Some Luftwaffe aces mistakenly believed that the P-38 was the easiest Allied fighter to shoot down in the North African theatre. This was perhaps due to the dark smoke that would pour out of the exhaust when the throttles were opened rapidly in an emergency and gave the impression of a crippled aircraft.

Captain James E. Pate, commander of the 27th FS, 1st FG, from 10 May to 3 September 1943 prepares for his final mission before returning to the US.

1st Lieutenant Lawrence P. Liebers, 96th FS, 82nd FG, talks with his crew chief while his armourer and assistant crew chief work on the aircraft. During his tour with the 96th FS, Liebers was credited with seven confirmed kills and five aircraft damaged. After the war Liebers stayed in the Air Force and was killed in a flying accident on 21 August 1946.

1st Lieutenant W.J. Hoelle of the 49th FS, 14th FG, based at Youks-les-Bains, Algeria, inspects damage to his P- 38 41-7665 *Maximum Goose* after he hit a telephone pole during a low level strafing mission in December 1942. According to *Life*: 'the blow tore a huge gash in the wing and flipped the plane on its back, but Hoelle righted it, returned home, got a new wing and was fighting again a few days later.' Hoelle commented: 'No plane has taken more criticism than the P-38, and to my mind no plane has more thoroughly demonstrated how unfair and uncalled for that criticism has been. The Lightning proved of inestimable value in the fighting in North Africa, and without any doubt it came as one of our most-effective all-round fighter planes... When we first arrived in North Africa, we thought the P-38 wouldn't work out well as a ground support airplane, but after seeing the results of concentrated firepower against trucks, columns and tanks, we knew we really had something.'

The inboard wing flap of a P-38 flown by 1st Lieutenant Herbert R. McQuown and 20-mm cannon damage. McQuown was hit in the leg by a bullet, which entered the cockpit and glanced off the instrument panel. He returned safely to base. Over the course of his tour, he was credited with two kills.

Combat damage to the right horizontal stabiliser of McQuown's P-38.

Hans Pichler, a German fighter ace with seventy-five confirmed aerial victories, recorded a frustrated P-38 intercept in his dairy: 'Over Tunisia, my flight encountered four P-38s and we slipped behind them, virtually unnoticed. Although our Gustavs [Bf 109Gs] gave all they could, the distance between us and the Lightnings hardly diminished. At a distance of about 500 metres I fired all my guns, but my shells exploded behind one of the P-38s. After several more ineffective bursts, the US pilots obviously sensed danger… Applying full war-emergency power, they disappeared, leaving us with our mouths wide open. The five-minute chase caused my engine to seize. One of the connecting rods pushed itself right through the cowling.'

1st Lieutenant Virgil H. Smith, 48th FS, 14th FG, was the first P-38 ace of the 12th Air Force. Seen here after his fifth kill on 12 December 1942, Smith was later KIA on 30 December while attempting to crash-land his damaged P-38F. A sixth aerial victory was not confirmed until after the war when he received full credit for shared kills early in his brief combat career. Several P-38 pilots in North Africa achieved the rare distinction of becoming 'aces in a day' by shooting down five or more enemy aircraft during one or more missions in a single day.

Colonel Troy Keith, commanding officer 14th FG, photographed just before take-off on a mission over Sicily. Lieutenant Harold Harper, 49th FS, recalled an incident at Telergma, Algeria involving Keith: 'An Arab chieftain came riding into our compound on a white horse, demanding payment for our use of the landing strip. If payment wasn't received he would graze his sheep and camels on the field. Our CO, Col. Troy Keith, replied that we would send up a P-38 and strafe any airstrip. He then sent an airplane up to make a few passes over the runway. The Arab thought better than to put his animals on the airstrip.'

A smiling Lieutenant Anthony 'Tony' Evans, P-38 Lightning Pilot, 14th FS, 14th FG, completed his fiftieth combat mission on 28 August 1943, escorting B-17s on mission to Terni, Italy. Evans was officially credited with four confirmed kills.

Another 14th FG pilot, Lieutenant Norman W. Jackson, who arrived in North Africa in December 1942, recalled arriving relatively green in the theatre: 'I had only thirty hours in P-38s, and no aerial gunnery… Arriving in North Africa, we were put in combat with the 14th FG at a time when they were being terribly mauled by ground fire as well as superior numbers of experienced German pilots. By the time I had 30 hours combat, I had bailed out, crashed landed in the desert, returned home on one engine, and brought another P-38 home so shot up that it was junked.'

Flight Officer H. Judson Hollock at the controls of a P-38 at an airbase near Tripoli, June 1943.

P-38s and P-51s arrive in Algeria still encased in a protective coating.

Almost 10,000 P-38 aircraft were manufactured by the end of the war. *Air Force* (February 1943) lauded the aircraft's versatility in North Africa. 'They do everything. They are used on air defense patrols of Allied strong points, over areas of concentrations, for ground strafing against troop columns and armoured equipment, for minimum altitude attacks against surface vessels, and for escorting heavy and medium bombers on missions. You can hardly find an assignment which P-38s cannot carry out. They escort our bombers 500 miles out and in – as far as the bombers go. They can carry two big bombs and drop them where they do the most good.'

Newly arrived P-38s at Maison Blanche, Algeria. The aircraft closest to the camera, construction number 3296, was P-38J serial number 43-28281.

P-38J, 42-104246, is assembled by men of the 36th Air Depot Group. Assigned to 48th FS, 14th FG, this aircraft was later lost in action on 12 May 1944 in combat forty miles south-east of Bologna, Italy. Killed in action was 2nd Lieutenant Herbert L. Aldrich. The 14th FG was taken out of combat on 28 January 1943. Out of the original fifty-four pilots who had flown in Operation Torch, thirty-two had been killed, twenty-three in combat. The FG was credited with sixty-two aircraft destroyed, seven probables and seventeen damaged.

Maintenance on the Allison engine of P-38F 43-28281. Regarding single engine operation, 1st Lieutenant W.J. Hoelle explained, 'Another criticism of the P-38 has been directed against its alleged inability to perform on a single engine. Nothing could be further from the truth. Such tales of single-engine operation caused apprehension among new pilots. When the engine quit on either side, the tendency is for the good engine to pull the plane over and into a spin. But this could be readily offset… I can readily cite a number of examples where P-38s came through combat on one engine, and did a good job of fighting the enemy at one time.'

P-38F 43-2136 (construction number 7163) 1st FG, 27th FS, pictured at Chateaudun-du-Rhumel Airfield, Algeria. This airfield was built by the US Army Corps of Engineers primarily as a heavy bomber airfield, complete with concrete runways, hardstands and taxiways. The 2nd BG and the 97th BG were the main tenants, flying B-17 Flying Fortress missions over targets in Italy, Tunisia, Sicily and Sardinia. P-38s of the 1st FG flew escort for the B-17s, as well as attacking targets of opportunity.

This P-38 of the 95th FS, 82nd FG, is positioned by a Cleveland Tractor Company 'Cletrac' M2 High Speed Tractor at a compass stop to obtain a true north compass reading. The aircraft's propellers counter-rotate – the right propeller clockwise, the left counter-clockwise. This feature eliminated torque and provided excellent climbing and diving characteristics. Pilots were trained to synchronise propellers by ear, using the tachometer and the Vernier throttle control.

Jumping on the tail of P-38G 42-12942 to help adjust the compass, a procedure known as 'swinging the compass'. This particular aircraft was assigned to John W. Weltman, CO of the 27th FS, 1st FG. It was coded HV-A, the first two letters being the 27th FS code. Weltman moved up to 1st FG headquarters as its executive officer in December 1942 and continued to fly 42-12942. In May 1943 he was transferred to the 82nd FG as its new CO, taking with him his trusty 42-12942. Weltman was awarded the Silver Star and later the Legion of Merit for service during the Korean War.

Damaged and wrecked P-38s parked in the salvage dump at Mediouna, Morocco, awaiting salvage of usable parts, April 1943.

Tail booms are examined in a P-38 boneyard. Note the Cletrac in the background.

P-38 destroyed in a German bombing raid on Maison Blanche on 18 November 1942.

The waterproof sealing is removed from partially assembled P-38s at Maison Blanche. 2nd Lieutenant Joseph F. Weber was killed on 8 October 1944 when flying P-38 42-104252 (right) in bad weather and crashing fifteen miles south-east of Triolo, Italy.

Tragedy at Biskra, 15 January 1943. 1st Lieutenant Elmer Hartman, 27th FS, penned in his diary: 'This afternoon a classmate, [1st Lieutenant Richard W.] McWherter in the 94th, was taking off with a flight of new boys on a practice mission and hit another ship on the runway taxiing. Threw him clear of the ship but killed him. Dust was so thick he couldn't see the other airplane.' McWherter, an experienced combat pilot with two victories to his credit, was a recipient of the Air Medal for 'an outstanding flight, a mass movement of single-seater air planes from July 4, 1942 to July 26, 1942, over an extremely hazardous, newly-established air route, including long over-water flights under very uncertain weather conditions.' He was posthumously awarded the DFC for 'extraordinary achievement'.

Chapter Three

Photographic Reconnaissance

A Lockheed F-5 of the 90th Photographic Wing (Reconnaissance) buzzes the coastal headquarters of an air base in North Africa. The 90th PW, which was activated in North Africa on 11 October 1943, provided photographic reconnaissance for the 12th and 15th Air Forces until reassigned on 1 October 1944. Two photographic reconnaissance versions of the P-38 were produced – the F4, based on the P-38E and F models, and the F-5, which was based on the P-38G and later models. This was

the most numerous version of the Photo Lightning. Approximately 23 per cent of all Lightnings were built as F-4 or F-5 photo reconnaissance aircraft. According to the P-38 Pilot's Training Manual: 'Pilots who fly F-5s come in sometimes at tree-top height, take their pictures, and are gone before enemy anti-aircraft guns can be trained on them. Or again, they come over at 30,000 feet and take pictures so clear that you can pick out automobile tyre tracks in the enlarged prints. Unarmed, and generally alone, these F-5s, because of their great range and tremendous speed, are among the finest photo-reconnaissance ships in the world.' Although listed as unarmed reconnaissance aircraft, some F-4 and F-5 variants were modified in the field to carry either two .50 calibre machine guns or two 20-mm cannons in the nose above the camera installation.

Dusty take off. The North African Campaign marked one of the first combat tests of aerial reconnaissance doctrine. Werner Von Fritsch, commander in chief of the German army from 1933 to 1938, predicted that the side with the best aerial photographic reconnaissance would ultimately win the war.

F-5A 42-13071 of the 12th Photo Reconnaissance Squadron, 3rd Photographic Reconnaissance Group photographed in a revetment. This aircraft later crashed into the Mediterranean, approximately 100 miles north of Bizerte, Tunisia, on 11 November 1943, killing pilot 1st Lieutenant Clifford E. Kent.

Captain Arthur D. Powers logs his flying time after returning from a photographic mission.

A photographic reconnaissance camera is installed. A twelve-inch camera at 20,000 feet produced a 1:20,000 scale image; a six-inch camera at the same altitude produced a 1:40,000 scale photo. For a smaller focal length camera to achieve a 1:20,000 scale, a pilot had to fly at 10,000 feet.

Personnel of the 90th Photographic Reconnaissance Wing unload camera magazines.

An army intelligence officer receives the exposed film from an F-5, likely P-38 42-13309 of the 12th PRS.

F-4 Lightnings of the 90th Photographic Wing (Reconnaissance). Activated on 22 November 1943, the Wing provided photographic reconnaissance for the 12th and 15th Air Forces until its groups were reassigned on 1 October 1944. As *Life* magazine explained, 'The easiest way to get into a P-38 is by climbing a 6-ft stepladder to the front of the wing and walking across the wing to the cockpit.'

Aerial photographs, according to the US Army Field Manual 30-21, *Military Intelligence – Role of Aerial Photography*, 1940, 'are one of the most important sources of information available to the commander…they are of paramount importance to all intelligence sections.'

Lockheed F-5A photographed on a reconnaissance mission.

Watching an F-5 taxi. Lightning pilots were taught that the 'airplane taxis easily. There is no danger of a nose-over or a groundloop if you find you must turn sharply or apply full brakes. You have unobstructed vision because the airplane is in a level attitude and you are surrounded by Plexiglas. Remember: there is no excuse for a taxi accident.'

Portraits of 90th Photographic Wing (Reconnaissance) pilots.

Pilots of the 90th Photographic Wing (Reconnaissance). Since they usually flew alone, their comrades rarely knew the cause should one fail to return.

The serial number visible on the left engine cowling (not visible) identifies this aircraft as Lockheed F- 5 s/n 42-13067, Major Leon W. Gray's aircraft. Note the 'camera' mission symbols. Other mission symbols on US aircraft, aside from bombs: swastikas including a broom (fighter sweep), umbrella (top cover), top hat and cane (fighter escort), parachute (paradrop), ships (enemy ship sunk) and Red Cross (medical evacuation mission). RAF and RAAF aircraft would sometimes display an ice cream for each mission over Italy.

Colonel Elliot Roosevelt, commanding officer of the 90th Photographic Wing (Reconnaissance) unit passes final instructions to one of his pilots, Lieutenant Colonel Frank L. Dunn at La Sénia (today Ahmed Ben Bella Airport), Algeria. Both men were recipients of the DFC for distinguished achievement in reconnaissance flying. Dunn's exploits featured in a November 1943 *Readers Digest* article: 'Frank Dunn's specialty was low obliques, where you come down to 100 feet and run like hell just over the water alongside an enemy beach while they pop it at you like a tin duck in a shooting gallery! You take pictures out the side window so the boys in the landing barges can have a panorama of the whole beach. "Dicing missions", the British call 'em. Because you gamble with your life, I guess.' 'Dunn has a rare sense of humour… One day they sent him to Cagliari in Sardinia. The weather was so heavy he had to dive in at very low altitude – and he came out right on top of an Axis airfield where a mess of planes were circling to land. Dunn says he didn't want to be conspicuous, so he circled too. They all eyed him, but they were so mixed up nobody fired, and finally he saw his chance to pull out over the city. He got to the railway station just as a train was coming in. He had some empty gas tanks it was time to jettison, and figuring to have a little fun, he came lower and cut them loose over the train… They came down with a hell of a clang on the roof of the car just back of the engine and Dunn could see the engineer bailing out of his cab, and most of the passengers through the windows.'

The morning of the photo reconnaissance mission: laboratory crew install and check the cameras while engineers insure the aircraft is mission ready.

Major Leon W. Gray, Dicer, pictured beside '67' (42-13067), which was shot down and ditched in the Adriatic on its 97th mission. Gray was saved by Air-Sea Rescue. After completing seventy-three missions, he returned to the US. His awards included the Air Medal with one oak leaf cluster, Air Medal with thirteen oak leaf clusters (two silver, three bronze), Distinguished Flying Cross with one oak leaf cluster, Distinguished Service Cross, Legion of Merit with one oak leaf cluster, Silver Star, World War II Victory Medal, Croix de Guerre (French), Distinguished Flying Cross (British), European-African-Middle Eastern Campaign Medal with one silver star and one bronze star. In 1950 Gray became commander of the now-closed Williams Air Force Base in Mesa, Arizona. He had a cameo role in the movie *Air Cadet*, starring a young Rock Hudson chronicling the life of cadets learning to become pilots. Gray died on 26 November 2007, aged 94.

Captain George W. Humbrecht pictured before a photo reconnaissance mission. Humbrecht was awarded both the US and British DFC for outstanding service.

59852 A.C

Algeria. Repairs to the engine of F-4, 41-1251. The F-4 was Lockheed's first photo reconnaissance variant of the P-38 Lightning. This was the fastest US fighter available at the beginning of the war. The original Army Air Corps proposal for the plane specified a speed greater than 360mph at altitudes of 20,000 feet using the 'most powerful engine' of the day, the Allison V-1710C. It was also envisaged that the aircraft would be equipped with the new General Electric turbo-superchargers then under development. This would provide the necessary performance at high altitude. A series of problems with later and more powerful Allison engines even prompted Lockheed engineers in 1941 to investigate replacing the troubled power plant with the Rolls-Royce Merlin 61. The British engine, had it been adopted, would have eliminated the need for turbo-superchargers and intercoolers, thereby simplifying engine installation and reliability. For a variety of reasons, including the tremendous pressure to produce the plane in quantity, the Allison engine was retained.

Weary after a long high-altitude mission, Captain Arthur D. Powers is free from the confines of the cockpit while exposed film canisters are retrieved for developing and analysis. A fundamental design flaw in the P-38's high altitude operations, especially in the European Theatre of Operations, was the lack of adequate cockpit heating. Often pilots would return from missions over Europe so numb that they required assistance to leave the aircraft.

This Canadian-built De Havilland F-8 Mosquito 43-324926, nicknamed *The Spook*, served with the 3rd Photo Group in North Africa. The aircraft, an early B.VII model, was originally KB 315 before its transfer to the USAAF. Part of the 32nd Squadron, 5th Pursuit Group, 12th AF, it joined F-4 Lightings in an aerial reconnaissance role. F8s usually carried additional fuel tanks in the bomb bay and featured Fairchild K.22 or K.17 cameras mounted in the nose and rear fuselage.

B-17F 42-24440, *I Got Spurs*, from the 3rd Photographic Reconnaissance and Mapping Group. The long-range reconnaissance-modified aircraft was nicknamed from a pair of silver spurs presented to Colonel Elliot Roosevelt by the citizens of Fort Worth, Texas.

Routine camera maintenance.

Members of the 90th Photographic Wing (Reconnaissance) analyse films. Inexperienced Army Air Force interpreters in North Africa naturally made mistakes analysing photographs. In one instance in March 1943 interpreters described the movement of fifty enemy tanks towards Allied lines west of Tunis. Only later did a subsequent analysis reveal that the tanks were in fact camels. The shortcomings of US observation units sent to North Africa led to an overhaul of the training system and the adoption of the British system during the summer of 1943.

Contact prints are prepared in a laboratory by the 90th Photographic Wing (Reconnaissance). Activated on 22 November 1943, the wing provided photographic reconnaissance for both the Twelfth and Fifteenth Air Forces.

Air Force personnel pore over photographs at a 90th Photographic Reconnaissance Wing air base 'somewhere in North Africa', 24 December 1942.

Comparison of objects at different scales on an aerial reconnaissance photo.					
Object	Actual Length	1:5,000	1:10,000	1:20,000	1:40,000
Foxhole	6 feet	0.0144 inches	0.0072 inches	0.0036 inches	0.0018 inches
Sd.Kfz. 124 – Wespe (10.5-cm self-propelled gun)	16 feet	0.0384 inches	0.0192 inches	0.0096 inches	0.0048 inches
Tiger I Tank	28 feet	0.0672 inches	0.0336 inches	0.0168 inches	0.0084 inches

Colonel Elliott Roosevelt (left) and General Eisenhower study aerial photographs of strategic points. In many ways, North Africa became the defining experience for the USAAF and set the stage for the future successes in Italy, France, and Germany. As operations in North Africa neared the end, many reconnaissance efforts shifted to Sicily and Italy.

Lieutenant General Carl A. Spaatz listens with interest to intelligence reports, 1 July 1943. *Air Force* magazine reported in its September 1945 issue that 'it was in Africa that tactical reconnaissance proved itself invaluable to the ground forces. At one point during the final stages of the drive on Tunis, when weather grounded reconnaissance operations, the ground commander flatly refused to move until his air photo coverage was obtained. Flying P-38s (F-versions), members of the 90th Photo Recon Wing experimented with night photography and brought low-level photo-recon missions – 'dicing' missions – to a state of development which was invaluable later on in Italy and still later in the battles of France and Germany. They got little recognition for their work – photo recon was strictly hush-hush in those days – but they came to be acknowledged as the real eyes of the army. To the long-range planners with an eventual D-day in mind, their work proved beyond question that complete photo coverage of the invasion area and its defenses would be indispensable to successful landings.'

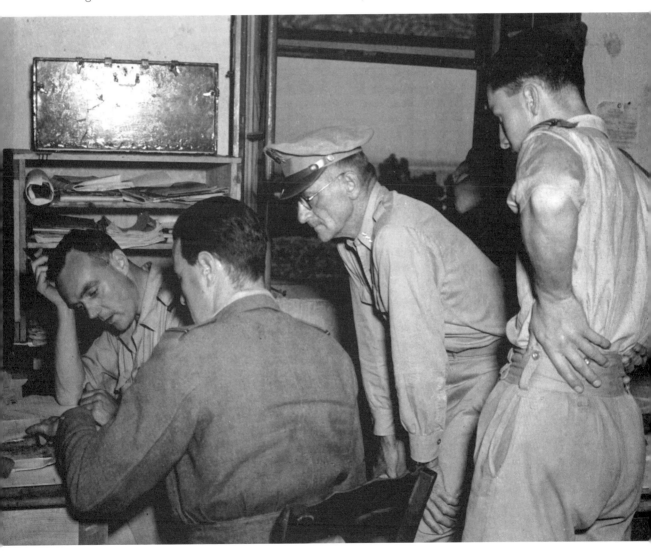

Chapter Four

Medium Bombers

North American B-25 Mitchell

B-25 pilots would read their aircraft's history in the instruction manual: 'You are going to fly a champ with a long line of firsts to her credit! First to see action on every fighting front. First Army airplane to sink an enemy sub. First medium bomber to fly from a carrier deck. First warplane to pack a 75-mm cannon. It all started when the Army asked for designs of a medium bomber to be submitted. That was on 25 January, 1939. Forty days later the B-25 was born! Daughter of a slide rule, with neither wind tunnel tests nor prototypes to study, the performance of the B-25 was a series of figures on an engineer's drawing board. Yet, 19 days after Hitler marched into Poland, in September 1939, the Army awarded the North American Aviation Company a contract for 148 Mitchell bombers, one of the largest orders written up to that time. In less than 2 months, following a number of modifications, the mock-up was approved. Exhaustive tests by Army engineers followed, and in August 1940, the first B-25 was test-flown and its performance found to be better than the claims its designers had made for it. Since that time hundreds of changes in design have been made, but the general appearance of all models of the B-25 has not changed. Designed to carry a bomb load of 3,500 lb. and a crew of 5, it has operated efficiently with heavier bomb loads and a crew of 6.'

As well as its two four-engined 'heavies', the US flew three medium bombers – the Martin B-26, the North American B-25 and the Douglas A-20 Havoc in North Africa. Pictured above are B-25s in close formation over the featureless North African desert. The closest aircraft to the camera is B-25C 41-13123 of the 82nd BS, 12th BG, dubbed *Old War Hoss Boo!*

B-25C 41-13193 of the 12th BG – a formation nicknamed the 'Earthquakers'. This was the first B-25-equipped formation to arrive in North Africa. Operations began from Egypt in mid-August 1942. In November the 310th and 391st BGs also arrived in North Africa, followed in March 1943 by the 321st and 340th BGs. The 12th BG later saw action in the invasions of Sicily and Italy before redeployment to the 10th Air Force in the China-Burma-India theatre.

A mixed Allied formation heads for the Axis-held Mareth Line in Tunisia on 9 January 1943. The closest aircraft, B-25C 41-12863, 82nd BS 12th BG, assigned to Captain Doug Spawn, was written off and consigned to salvage on 19 April 1943. Note the US manufactured Baltimore IIIs (supplied under the Lend-Lease program) of RAF 232 Wing in the background.

Pre-flight. The B-25 Mitchell was named in honour of William 'Billy' Mitchell, one of America's firmest advocates of air power.

B-25C pictured in the midst of a Western Desert sandstorm. The original caption states: 'With the wind blowing and sand flying in every direction, getting into motors, into food, and in your hair, is the climatic conditions under which our boys must operate. These storms however do not stop the continual bombing missions, and these "Earthquakers" take off at regular intervals to give Mr Schikelgruber's boys a taste of their own medicine.' In March 1944, the 12th BG was awarded the Presidential Unit Citation: 'For outstanding performance of duty in action against the enemy in direct support of the British Eighth Army in the Middle East Campaign from the battle of El Alamein to the capitulation of the enemy forces in Tunisia and in Sicily. This group operating from advanced landing fields directly behind the front lines under the most difficult of weather and terrain conditions, carried out continuous and devastating bombing raids against enemy airdromes, ground installations, troops, and supply lines as well as repeated aerial engagements with enemy aircraft. The airplane crews of this organisation exhibited the greatest bravery and resourcefulness, while its ground personnel, in the face of repeated enemy attacks, performed all duties with utter disregard for their personal safety. By the superior courage, initiative, untiring efforts, and devotion to duty of all personnel of this organisation, despite personal hardships and the most difficult and hazardous of conditions, the 12th Bombardment Group (M) contributed greatly to the defeat of the enemy in the Middle East in keeping with the highest traditions of the United States Army.'

'Sand still blowing. Missions called off.'

The ferocity of a sandstorm was recorded by Sergeant Sidney Christophersen, 434th BS, 12th BG, in his wartime diary dated 28 March 1943: 'No missions today – takeoff would have been impossible – the worst sand and windstorm we have encountered – blew down the seven mess tents, operations, supply armament and about half of the rest of the camp.'

B-25s, 83rd BS, 12th BG, in formation over Tunisia.

Closest to camera is B-25C 41-13195 *Desert Vagabond Jnr.*, 83rd BS, 12th BG.

B-25 C 41-13070 *Shanghai-Lil* of the 310th BG photographed over Berteaux, Morocco (above) and low over the Mediterranean (below). Wrote Frank B. Hawkins, B-25 pilot from the 381st BS, 310th BG: 'We are moved again after a bombing raid on Tunis today. What a job it is flying formation at 265 MPH.'

B-25C 42-53460 *Sand Blower* forms the backdrop to a 9th AF Easter Service, 1943. During the war the Pope gave special dispensation to allow afternoon mass for US troops serving abroad.

Berteaux, Morocco. B-25s of the 310th BG taxiing before take-off. The closest aircraft is B-25C 41-13071.

2nd Lieutenant Albert R. Walcott, as the original caption states, demonstrates lesson one on 'how not to behave in this theatre'.

Captain James T. Holley and crew from *Seasweep*, 438th BS, 310th BG, relax after completing fifty missions. The BG's official history noted in October 1943 that thirteen officers and fifteen enlisted men had completed fifty combat missions. 'No crews have been sent to replace them. Our planes are becoming old and mission weary, and some of them need to be replaced. This is true also of much of our ground equipment and some of our ground personnel.'

Captain Ralph M. Lower, pilot, and his crew of decorated B-25 *Desert Warrior* of the 82nd BS, 12th BG, pictured before their return to the US. Note the map under the cockpit window recording mission targets. The medium bomber flew in seventy-three combat missions in operations from El Alamein through to Sicily, dropping seventy tons of bombs and downing two enemy fighters. Half a century later turret gunner James 'Pat' Garofalo recalled: 'We learned some things then, the hard way, that our airmen use today against Iraq. For example, we discovered that our 250-pound anti-personnel bombs burrowed into the sand before exploding and thus dissipated much of their force. To correct this, we attached three-feet of pipe to the bomb's nose so it would explode at ground level. It worked very well. Now the Air Force has bombs with timed fuses.' In 2012, a 93-year-old Lower recollected part of the War Bond tour: 'We visited gasoline refineries that were under construction. We'd put the airplane on display and talk to the workers building refineries, telling them how badly we needed that gasoline overseas.'

'Somewhere in the Western Desert', B-25 crew. Left to Right: Sergeant G.H. Cornwall; Sergeant B. Kuhlman; 2nd Lieutenant Bob Hill, Clear Lake, Iowa; 1st Lieutenant Bill Brytan, unknown; 2nd Lieutenant Jack Cross.

B-25C 41-13078 *Wolf Pack* of the 380th BS, 310th BG.

Staff Sergeant R.E. Dowling, 380th BS, 310th BG, attaches fuses to 500 lb bombs for B-25 *Wolf Pack* before a raid. March 1943, Berteaux airfield.

Homeward bound after fifty missions, B-25 *Shanghai-Lil*, 428th BS, 310th BG. Captain John H. Beatty and crew will now leave North Africa for a Stateside War Bonds tour. Beatty completed this last mission on 21 September 1943 against Caserta in Italy. According to the squadron diary, Beatty 'was one of the oldest pilots we had from point of service, and perhaps one of the best. His plane was the first medium bomber to land on North African soil in the early days of the war [20 November 1942].' Beatty was recommended for the Air Medal and eight oak leaf clusters.

A B-25C is readied for a mission.

Another 'Earthquaker' – B-25C 41-13167 *Pluto* of the 12th BG.

Having undertaken fifty-two combat missions, Captain LaVerne B. Johnson's B-25D *Stud*, 379th BS, 310th BG, is ready for the return journey to the US and a tour across the country selling War Bonds. Standing in the nose is 1st Lieutenant Donald C. Biggs; below him sits Captain Johnson. L to R on top of the bomber: 1st Lieutenant Willard E. Wilvert, Staff Sergeant Herman E. Keller, Technical Sergeant William H. Etheridge, Technical Sergeant Issac Rousso. Sitting in the pilot's seat: Captain James R. Holstead. As early as Autumn 1943, Colonel Malcolm C. Grow, Eighth Air Force surgeon, urged that combat crews in Europe be relieved from operational duty after fifteen missions. Major General Ira C. Eaker, Eighth Air Force, afterwards announced that the tour of duty of bomber crews would be a minimum of 25 missions, and for fighter pilots, 150 missions or 200 hours of operational flying hours.

Private Robert B. Carlson of the 310th BG refuels a B-25 with a 4,000-gallon refilling unit at Berteaux, March 1943. Partly visible is the upper gun turret, which was located just forward of the armour plate bulkhead that separated the radio compartment from the photographer's and tail observer's compartment. The turret was equipped with two .50 calibre M-2 machine guns that could be rotated 360 degrees.

1st Lieutenant Samuel C. Schlitzkus, B-25 pilot, prepares 'to give the enemy its daily dose of bad medicine.' On his 19th mission, 5 June 1943, Schlitzkus and crew aboard B-25C 42-32413 were shot down by an enemy fighter while bombing enemy gun positions on Pantelleria. After making a controlled landing at sea and exiting the aircraft, the crew were machine-gunned. Staff Sergeant Alvin I. Langford was killed. Schlizkus survived to lead a long and illustrious flying career. He was awarded the Distinguished Flying Cross, Air Medal with four Oak Leaf Clusters, the Commendation Medal and the Purple Heart. As well as being captured and held as a PoW for nearly two years, he ferried General Mark Clark to the Casablanca Conference in 1943, attended by Churchill, Roosevelt and Stalin. After the war he was appointed Commander of the Air Element for aerial photography during the atomic tests on Eniwetok, South Pacific in 1954. Schlitzkus died on 13 September 2002, aged 82.

Staff Sergeant Alvin I. Langford, 428th BS, 310th BG, achieved his fifth victory – a German Bf 109 – on his 28th mission aboard B-25C 41-13094 *Seasweep*. When asked about the victory, the upper turret gunner replied, 'You don't have time to think about anything but knocking them down.'

Upper turret showing the damage to the gun sight from an encounter with three German fighters. The gunner, purportedly shot in the eye, kept firing and downed one, possibly two, of the enemy attackers. The B-25 pilot's manual expounded how the gunners 'must be thoroughly familiar with the machine guns. They should know how to maintain the guns, how to clear jams and stoppages, and how to harmonise the sights with the guns…. Keep your gunners' interest alive at all times. Any form of competition among the gunners themselves should stimulate their interest.'

B-25C 41-12963 *Missouri Waltz* 446th BS, 321st BG. L to R standing: 2nd Lieutenant Theodore C. Wright, 2nd Lieutenant Sterling Davis, 1st Lieutenant James L. Bradley. Front: 2nd Lieutenant Benjamin W. Anzalone, Staff Sergeant Alfred A. Rockafellow.

Fifty missions completed. Crew and mascot beside B-25C 41-13201, *Poopsie*, of the 445th BS, 321st BG.

The camp artist is kept busy making changes as new ideas emerge.

A serving of coffee and donuts for the crew of B-25C 41-13123 *Old War Hoss Boo*! Note the RAF flashes and the metal patches repairing combat damage. This aircraft was declared 'non-operational' in April 1944.

Algeria. Pilot Lieutenant James I. Miller (standing 2nd from right) and his crew are congratulated by Colonel Anthony G. Hunter, commander of the 310th BG (standing on Miller's right) after completing the group's 2,000th sortie. Note the three vessels sunk.

A B-25 bomber crew check their flight plans before taking off. They are (left to right) Lieutenant Bob Hill, bombardier; Lieutenant Bill Brytan, pilot; Lieutenant Jack Cross, navigator (checking his watch); and Lieutenant Don Castle, co-pilot; the crew member in rear is unidentified.

Most Reverend Francis J. Spellman, Archbishop of New York, poses with a B-25 crew in Tunisia, 1943. Spellman, who was appointed Catholic vicar of the United States Armed Forces in 1939, worked to mobilise Catholics behind the war effort.

Members of the 428th BS, 310th BG, await the presentation of the Purple Heart by Colonel Anthony G. Hunter at Berteaux, 9 March 1943. According to the Group diary, few combat missions were flown in March since the 'weather continued to be cold and windy, with frequent showers which kept the ground perpetually damp and soggy.' The combat crews were also sent away for a rest…a fleet of C-47s departed from Berteaux, with all the 301th combat crew-members who had participated in five or more missions. They were bound for a rest camp high in the mountains of Morocco, near the Sultan's summer palace.'

Major General James 'Jimmy' Doolittle at the controls of B-25 *Baby*, 379th BS, 310th BG, at Heliopolis airport, Egypt 1943. Doolittle had earlier chosen the B-25 as the best plane to lead the famous surprise attack on Tokyo following Japan's entry into the war and a string of victories over the Allies. From the deck of the carrier USS Hornet, then Colonel Doolittle, aboard B-25 40-2344, led sixteen bombers on what became known as the 'Doolittle Raid'. The morale-boosting mission demonstrated that Japan was vulnerable to air attack and served as a retaliatory response to the Pearl Harbor attack. In May 2014 the US House of Representatives awarded a Congressional Gold Medal to the airmen for 'outstanding heroism, valor, skill, and service to the United States in conducting the bombings of Tokyo.'

Doolittle led air operations on the European, North African and Pacific fronts, receiving a promotion to lieutenant general in 1944. He commanded the 8th Air Force, his largest command, in 1944–45. He retired from Air Force Reserve duty in February 1959. Doolittle received the Presidential Medal of Freedom in 1989. He died at the age of 96 on 27 September 1993 and is buried at Arlington National Cemetery, Virginia.

General Gilbert X. Cheves, Chief of Staff, US Army Forces in the Middle East, and two members of the Air Staff, Washington welcome Doolittle upon his arrival. L to R: Colonel Sol A. Rosenblatt, General J. Doolittle, General G. Cheves and Colonel Clarence S. Irvine. After the war Irvine broke several aviation records. On 11 December 1945 he set a record for flying from Burbank, California, to Floyd Bennett Field, New York, in 5 hours, 27 minutes aboard B-29B 44-84061 (a light-weight variant of the B-29 Superfortress) *Pacusan Dreamboat*. In October 1946 Irvine completed the first non-stop flight over the North Pole. His forty-hour flight in the same B-29 began in Hawaii and ended in Egypt. During the Korean War build-up, Irvine became deputy commander of the Air Materiel Command for Production and Weapons Systems. His task was to oversee the introduction of new jet bombers and fighters into the combat units with particular emphasis on the B-47 and B-52 bombers. Irvine retired from the Air Force in the 1950s as a US Air Force Lieutenant General. He died on 7 September 1975 and is buried at Arlington National Cemetery.

A squadron artist at work on the 'nose art' of a B-25C from the 12th BG, the 'Earthquakers'. Regulations on such art were relaxed, even ignored during the Second World War. Pin-ups were a dominant theme, as were cartoon characters and the names of hometowns and states. The names of wives, girlfriends and fiancées were common expressions of affection. Strict rules now apply and all nose art suggestions must be vetted and approved. A 2015 US Air Force memorandum states that nose art must be 'distinctive, symbolic, gender neutral, intended to enhance unit pride, designed in good taste.'

B-25C 41-13071, 310th BG, during an overhaul by members of the 346th Service Squadron at Berteaux, Algeria.

Algiers. B-25 41-12926 *Hawkeye*, 448th BS, 321st BG, piloted by 1st Lieutenant John C. Stewart was intercepted by a Bf 109 on a 3 July 1943 mission to bomb Alghero, Sardinia. Damage was sustained to the right rudder, wing, fuselage and engine nacelle. Staff Sergeant Raymond A. Morris shot down the enemy fighter. The regular pilot of the bomber, 1st Lieutenant Leland A. Moore and his bombardier 2nd Lieutenant Raymond G. Petrich look on as repair crew work on the aircraft. Records show that Moore was next at the controls of the aircraft on a 14 July raid on Messina and a 16 July raid on the Vibo Valentia aerodrome. Lieutenant Stewart completed his fifty-mission tour of combat duty in October 1943.

Examining flak damage.

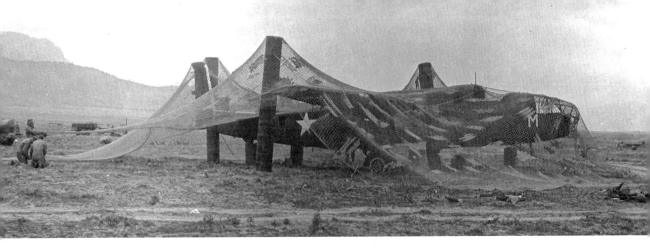

February 1943. US Army engineers cover a derelict B-25C with camouflage netting. Parts from the bomber have already been salvaged, such as the outboard flap, to keep other B-25s airworthy.

Algiers. 1st Lieutenant Earl L. Stutts, 380th BS, 310th BG, examines combat damage to his B-25. Stutts was reported missing in action on 25 July 1943. The operations order before the flight read: 'In compliance with verbal orders, Commanding Officer, B-25D aircraft 41-30388 and crew listed below will, on or about 25 July 1943 proceed on a local test hop for the purpose of checking major repair on left wing.' Crew: Pilot – 1st Lieutenant, Earl L. Stutts; Navigator – 2nd Lieutenant Charles M. Head; Engineer – Staff Sergeant Alfred S. Jensen. The 380th BS diary recorded the tragedy: 'While testing his plane, Lieut. Stutts was unable to bring the ship out of a test dive and crashed into the sea off Tabarka.' Major James F. Gavin was an eyewitness to the crash: 'At about 1000 hours July 25th, a pink coloured B-25 was seen flying low over the beach at Tabarka. After two or three trips up and down the beach, the airplane flew toward Rome, gaining altitude. A turn was made and the airplane was then flying east at about 8,000 to 10,000 feet altitude. When about five miles off the Tabarka lighthouse, there was a change in the sound of the engines and the airplane went into a dive and then a spin. Two or three turns were made before it hit the water. No parachutes were seen to leave the airplane. A large geyser of water was seen when the airplane hit the water, but no wreckage was visible.'

This B-25, nicknamed *Cobra*, was hit by flak during a sweep over Tunis and made a forced landing. It will end its days in salvage.

Algiers. Flying Officer W.E. Cook and crew of B-25C 42-64574 310th BG, 381st BS, examine combat damage from a raid on Gerbini (Sicily) on 12 July 1943. The squadron diary recorded: 'F/O Cook's aircraft was so badly damaged by enemy fighters and flak that S/Sgt. Lichtenstein and Sgt. Powell, radio-gunner and upper turret gunner, bailed out near our lines. S/Sgt. Lichtenstein and Sgt. Powell returned to the Squadron at 15:30 on 15 July 1943 with the following story: 'The flak had punched big hole in the fuselage, the lower turret was knocked out by an explosive shell, part of the tail was missing, and Sgt Powell had been thrown out of the turret with a piece of flak in his heel and another just below the knee, plus about thirty cuts and scratches on his legs. Sgt. Lichtenstein received three minor flak cuts and hurt his knee. Powell was momentarily dazed, so Lichtenstein helped him on with his 'chute and then bailed out. Looking around, Powell saw the open hatch and no radio operator, and decided he would hit the silk too. (F/O Cook had not sounded the alarm nor ordered them to jump.) On the way down a Me-109 banked over towards Lichtenstein, but a Spit took care of the situation—decisively.'

A wrecked B-25C is lifted onto a flat-bed trailer to be transported to a salvage depot in Berteaux, North Africa. March 1943. The truck is an Autocar U-7144-T Tractor, 4-ton, 4x4.

With the last bolts and connections severed, the high outer wing of a B-25 is removed from the main inner section with the aid of a mobile crane for later reissue. A 1943 9th Air Force publication lauded the USAAF mechanics serving in North Africa, who 'don't get medals or newspaper headlines. Their reward must come from the certain knowledge that without them many a ship would not fly. A spirit as gritty as the sand about them sustained these soldiers through long night vigils and daily grinds. Battered planes limping home have taken to the air again the following day after their over-night miracles of rejuvenation.'

The end of the road for B-25D 41-29764 *Montana Sheep Herder*, 446th BS, 321st BG. The veteran of 21 missions is being carted to the 15th AAF salvage yard to be dismantled, sent to the 'bone yard' and used for reclaimed parts.

Bone yard entrance. Note the 15th AAF sign that appears to be affixed to a B-17 tail gun section.

Douglas A-20 Havoc

Douglas A-20B 41-3171 *Lady Jean*, 47th BG 12th AF, belly-landed on 16 January 1943 at Youks-les-Bains, Algeria. Damaged by flak, the light bomber returned with one wing bomb still attached.

1st Lieutenant C.W. Gustafson adds another combat mission star to his A-20. A total of five A-20 squadrons operated in North Africa. Initially, the same low level tactics were used as in the Pacific, but German anti-aircraft fire was far more effective than its Japanese equivalent and losses were unacceptably high. The squadrons accordingly were forced to undertake less accurate but safer medium level operations.

The Martin B-26 Marauder

The US Air Corps literally bought the B-26 from the Glenn L. Martin Company off the drawing board in 1939. A production contract was signed in September of that year. The first aircraft flew in November 1940. After a rocky start through a number of training accidents, the Marauder gained a reputation as a 'widow maker'. It was derided with such nicknames 'The Baltimore Whore' and 'The Flying Prostitute' in reference to the aircraft's short wingspan and little visible means of support! Design improvements and effective combat techniques, however, led to the B-26 Marauder becoming one of the finest medium bombers of the war. Former B-26 pilot and retired Air Force Captain James Vining recalled: 'It was not the airplane I wanted to fly. I was horrified because of all the bad stories I had heard about the B-26 Marauder. I'd heard all kinds of things – for example, I'd heard you couldn't fly it on one engine so if an engine went out on take-off you would crash… I learned that in its early days the B-26 produced more than its share of problems, but the real reason for its poor reputation was inexperienced instructors. And the B-26 may have gone to war prematurely. It did well in the Pacific. It had a few defects: the Curtiss Electric propeller would run away. They never changed the propeller. They just worked out the details. As for the instructors, they beefed up and expanded the training program – which was never as bad as people thought – and it improved.'

Staff Sergeant Clifford R. Wherley, a 16-year-old five-foot-five-inch turret gunner with 21 missions over enemy territory and recipient of the Air Medal and three Oak Leaf Clusters, is seen before heading home to the US where he was honourably discharged. As a 14-year-old, Wherley had watched a movie about Sergeant York, one of the most decorated US army soldiers of the First World War. The next morning, at 4 am, he slipped out of his parent's Illinois home, caught a bus for Peoria and enlisted on 1 April 1942. After his discharge Wherley worked in a factory that produced B-26 bombers and for the Caterpillar Tractor Co before re-enlisting in the Navy and serving again as a B-26 turret gunner, this time in the Pacific. He retired from the military at the age of 19 in 1946. Considered to be the youngest American to have served in the war, Wherley died in 2013 at the age of 85.

A flight of Marauders from the 440th BS, 319th BG, takes to the air. A trademark of the 319th BG was their six-abreast group take-offs, a procedure that saved time and fuel while forming up. The problem of desert sand, however, halted the practice until the unit was moved to Decimomannu, Sardinia, at the beginning of November 1943.

Four B-26s of the 320th BG prepare to take off on a mission from an airfield in Berteaux, Algeria, March 1943. 'Operations in extremely hot weather,' attested the pilot's manual, 'offers little difficulty. Remember that your takeoff run is longer. Avoid overheating on the ground. Be sure that cylinder-head temperatures do not exceed 220°C before starting takeoff.' But as a former pilot wrote, 'Except for Western Desert bases of combat units, runway length averaged 4,000 feet, not enough for the ground-loving Martin B-26 when the temperature was 120°[F] in the shade. Runway overruns bore grim proof that ignoring the thermometer was dangerous to your health.'

From an advanced base in Tunisia, the original wartime caption states, 'B-26 Marauders head for a target in Italy. Marauder pilots were instructed in the benefits of formation flying: 'When you get to combat you will find that your best insurance for becoming a veteran of World War II is a good, well-planned, well-executed formation. Formation flying is just about everything in combat. Groups which are noted for their efficiency in formation flying are usually well-known for their low casualty rate and their effective operations. A properly flown formation affords you many advantages and much better protection. Controlled firepower, manoeuvrability and movement of a number of aircraft, concentrated bombing pattern, better fighter protection – these are some of the desirable things which good formations provide.' Moreover, 'There is no place among combat outfits for primadonnas. There is no place for a man who questions authority, fails to obey orders in the air, or who practises rugged individualism in flight. He endangers not only his own life, but the lives of many others, as well as valuable equipment.'

B-26B 41-17841 *Fertile Myrtle*, 437th BS, 319th BG, at Biskra. This Marauder was destroyed after six Ju 88s bombed the southern Algerian airfield on 3 January 1943.

Technical Sergeant Leo E. Walker (engineer-crew chief) checks the 2,000 hp Pratt & Whitney R-2800 Double Wasp radial engine of B-26C 41-31584 *Zero-4*, 437th BS, 319th BG during a lull in operations. The aircraft would complete 148 combat missions; Walker was later awarded the Croix de Guerre with Palm by the French Government for precision attacks on bridges in support of the French ground forces in Italy.

Martin B-26 bombers of the 319th BG pictured at the desert airfield at Biskra, Algeria. Note the B-17 in the centre. Arriving at the 'oasis town', intelligence officer Lieutenant Colonel Clyde W. Gabler noted in his diary that Biskra was a 'French army garrison town, home of the 6th Spahis Cavalry Regiment, native Algerian troops with French officers. Well-trained and disciplined, they took up the duty of perimeter guards for the airfield.'

Testament to the damage a Marauder could sustain, B-26B 41-17747 *Earthquake McGoon*, 37th BS, 17th BG is shown returning to Algeria with extensive flak damage to the left wing and No. 1 engine nacelle. 2nd Lieutenant Franklin P. Bedford in the bomber's astrodome surveys the damage. The aircraft belly-landed at Telergma Airfield on 23 March 1943. None of the crew were injured. Top Turret Gunner Technical Sergeant Robert R. Rapp later recalled: After we completed the bomb run and left our formation, Lieutenant Bedford crawled back to take a look at the damage that the anti-aircraft had done. When he got back up front, he told us on the intercom that our system was shot up. I knew then it was hydraulic fluid and not gasoline that was streaming back from the wing. When we finally limped back to our base, we circled the area around the field a few times and then Lieutenant Bedford told us the news. "Men," he said, "our hydraulic system was shot out and our landing gear won't come down, so I'm going to belly-land this ship. Now, you can go in with me on the belly landing or you can bail out." Almost in unison we all said, "We're going to belly in with you." I, personally, felt much safer riding in with Lts. Bedford and May than parachuting out. They were couple of cool pilots. Bedford told us to throw everything out that wasn't bolted down and sit against the bulkhead. Lts. Bedford and May brought *Earthquake McGoon* in on the belly smoother than anyone could expect, and before the dust could settle, we were out of there and a hundred yards away.'

Ordnance crews at a 15th AAF Marauder base – the so-called 'Boomerang Bombers' because of their ability to return from the most difficult missions – celebrate the milestone of 8,000,000 lbs of bombs dropped on Axis forces. Over 5,000 B-26s were produced. Despite early misgivings, it had the lowest attrition rate of any US aircraft in the 9th Air Force.

B-26B 41-17903 *Hell Cat* and crew pose for a photograph to commemorate the first B-26 to complete fifty combat missions. Note the names of the crew inscribed on the nose.

Lieutenant Colonel Eugene Fletcher presents Captain Clarence A. Kirley, B-26 pilot, with the Distinguished Flying Cross. The award was given for 'extraordinary achievement while participating in aerial flight in the North African Theatre of Operations as pilot of a B-26 type aircraft. On 14 September 1943, while piloting the lead plane of a formation of thirty-six medium bombers, flying ground support of the Fifth Army at Salerno, Captain Kirley's plane was hit in both engines by intense anti-aircraft fire just as he reached the initial point. Realising the vital importance of the target and the formation's dependence on his lead plane, Captain Kirley courageously determined to continue the long bomb run before seeking personal safety. Through the concentrated anti-aircraft barrage, Captain Kirley steadied his crippled plane long enough to accomplish great damage to numerous enemy installations and to the Auletta Road Junction through which German troops were being evacuated from the Potenza area. Then, with one engine feathered and the other pouring oil and sputtering, he successfully brought his crew and plane to safety in Sicily.' Kirley's aircraft was B-26B 41-18189 *Dusty's Devil*. The aircraft in the background is B-26B 41-43272 *Hawkeye*.

A B-26 crew, according to the original wartime caption, look 'thankfully at the left engine that recovered from a severe coughing case after being attacked by German Messerschmitts in a raid over Sardinia.' The B-26 pilot was trained in crew morale in addition to flying skills: 'As airplane commander you are responsible for the daily welfare of every man in your crew. See that they are properly quartered and clothed and fed. Away from home, help them temporarily if they run short of funds. In brief, they are your crew, a little specialised army all your own, and their physical and mental well-being is your responsibility… You are responsible for seeing that your team is capable of safe, efficient and successful conduct on all missions during training and combat operation. Supervise the training of the team both on the ground and in the air. Check their progress constantly… Never forget that you are preparing your crew for combat. You are responsible for every man's ability to do his job in the best possible manner. To do this, you have to extend your leadership over your crew's every activity.'

Major General James H. Doolittle poses before a B-26 at Maison Blanche, October 1943. Doolittle had earlier quelled complaints about the medium bomber that it was too unforgiving for the average pilot and recommended that it stay in production. In his memoirs, he recollected: 'The word was out that it was a "killer," and I suspect that many crew members were convinced that they could never survive the war in that airplane, not because of the enemy but because they would meet their maker in a noncombat accident.' As an aside, the B-26 pilot's manual warned: 'Always stop with the nosewheel straight… If the nosewheel isn't straight, the strut may break off when you apply power.'

February 1943. B-26B, 41-17809, *Gimszy Inc. Bombs & Bullets* awaits salvage somewhere in North Africa after crash landing due to flak damage. The bomber belonged to the 34th BS, 17th BG, 12th AF.

Ground personnel beside a B-26 from the 319th BG, 12th AF, inside a hangar at Oran Tafraoui, Algeria. Note the aircraft's missing rudder.

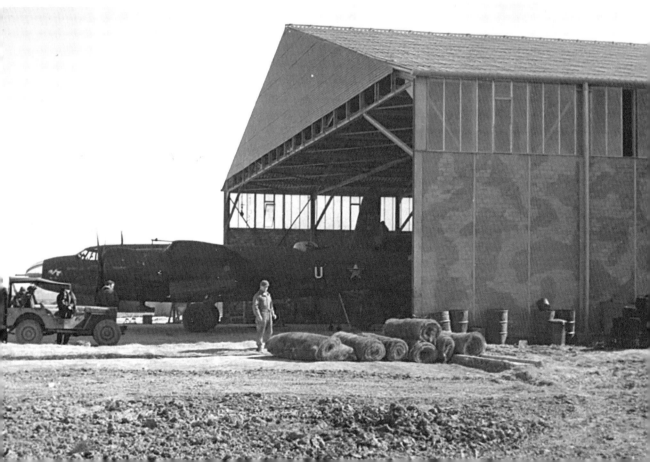

Chapter Five

The 'Heavys'

B-17 Flying Fortress

The United States operated two heavy bombers in North Africa: the Boeing B-17 Flying Fortress and the Consolidated B-24 Liberator. Both were all metal, four engine, long-range bombers armed with up to thirteen machine guns. The B-17 was the older of the two aircraft, its prototype having first flown on 28 July 1935.

Men of the 43rd Service Group are pictured refuelling the two B-17s below. Closest to the camera is B-17F 42-3146 of the 20th BS, 2nd BG. The B-17F measured 74 feet 9 inches (22.8 metres) long with a wingspan of 103 feet, 9.4 inches (31.6 metres) with an overall height of 19 feet, 1 inch (5.2 metres). From an empty weight of 34,000 pounds (15.4 tons), its maximum take-off weight was 56,500 pounds (25.6 tons). With a normal fuel load of 2,520 gallons (9,540 litres), the B-17F had a maximum range of 2,880 miles (4,635 kilometres). Armed with a 6,000-pound (2.7 ton) bomb load, the bombers range was reduced to 1,300 miles (2,092 kilometres).

B-17F 42-30314 *Beautiful Baby*, 353rd BS, 301st BG, photographed taxiing at Oujda, French Morocco, in June 1943. Three US companies manufactured the B-17F: 2,000 by Boeing in Seattle, 605 by Douglas at Long Beach and 500 by Lockheed-Vega. The B-17F was first model to be flown in large numbers by the USAAF. Armed with up to thirteen .50-calibre machine guns, it had a range of 2,000 miles and a bomb capacity in excess of 8,000 pounds.

Crewmembers of the 301st BG clean their B-17 at Biskra, Algeria in December 1942. Following its activation in the US in February 1942, the 301st BG was transferred to the United Kingdom in July 1942. After flying eight missions (104 sorties, dropping 186 tons of bombs and losing one aircraft between September to November 1942) it was assigned to the 12th Air Force and moved to North Africa in November 1942. A year later the group was transferred to the 15th Air Force in Italy where it flew in support of the invasion of Southern France (Operation Dragoon) in August 1944.

Manufactured by Lockheed-Vega, B-17 F 42-5782 *High Tension* originally flew with the 2nd BG. Seen here minus armament, it is possibly serving as a 'hack' aircraft in the 483rd BG.

A B-17 crew pose for a picture beside their aircraft. Note the Bugs Bunny motif and 'Texan' written under the waist gunner's position. A 1943 B-17 pilot training manual advised: 'Train your crew as a team. Keep abreast of their training. It won't be possible for you to follow each man's courses of instruction, but you can keep a close check on his record and progress. Get to know each man's duties and problems. Know his job, and try to devise ways and means of helping him to perform it more efficiently. Each crew member naturally feels great pride in the importance of his particular specialty. You can help him to develop his pride to include the manner in which he performs that duty. To do that you must possess and maintain a thorough knowledge of each man's job and the problems he has to deal with in the performance of his duties.' Typical B-17F and G models carried ten-man crews: Four officers (pilot, co-pilot, bombardier and navigator) and six enlisted men (engineer/top turret gunner, two waist gunners, ball turret gunner, tail gunner and radio operator).

A Combat box or 'staggered formation' of B-17s. This tactical three-plane formation was designed to maximise the defensive firepower of the bombers' machine guns. *Life* reported in March 1943 how 'Every sunny morning formations of U.S bombers rise like desert condors from the airfields of Algeria and head for enemy skies. Sometimes they soar south-westward and unload their bombs over Rommel's supply bases at Gabes, Sousse and Sfax. Sometimes they cross the blue Mediterranean and hit Italians in Naples, Sardinia or Sicily. But most often they sail straight for the twin cities of the North African coast – Tunis and Bizerte.'

A combat camera unit records the arrival of B-17s as they return to Tunisia from a mission in the Mediterranean theatre. Journalist *Ernie Pyle* described such a homecoming: 'It was late afternoon at our desert airdrome. The sun was lazy, the air was warm, and a faint haze of propeller dust hung over the field, giving it softness. It was time for the planes to start coming back from their mission, and one by one they did come – big Flying Fortresses and fiery little Lightnings.'

Stills from the 1943 US training film *Bombers over North Africa* showing bombers of 321st and 97th bomb groups operating over Tunisia. Produced by the US Army Air Forces Motion Picture Service Department, the nineteen-minute film depicts aircraft preparation, briefing of the crews by intelligence officers, a bombing raid, and later interrogation of the crews upon their return. B-17F 41-24370 *Berlin Sleeper II* (above) was the first bomber in the MTO to complete 100 missions. The 97th BG left bases in England on 9 November following the launch of Operation Torch a day earlier. Upon arrival, the group was passed from the 8th to the 12th Air Force.

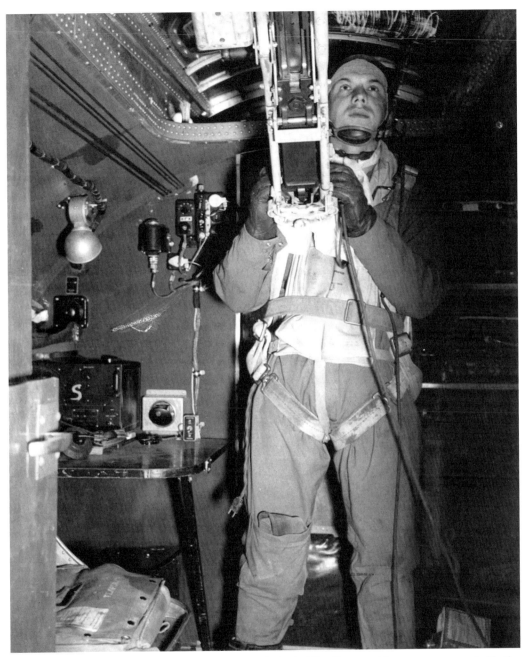

The B-17 radio operator was an also an air gunner. A single .50 calibre machine gun was mounted in the radio compartment to fire through the top hatch opening. The 1943 pilot training manual explained: 'In addition to being a radio operator, the radio man is also a gunner. During periods of combat he will be required to leave his watch at the radio and take up his guns. He is often required to learn photography… The radio operator who cannot perform his job properly may be the weakest member of your crew – and the crew is no stronger than its weakest member.' Sergeant J.M. Drabant poses for the picture. After a long raid, gunners would find themselves ankle-deep in spent brass bullet casings.

Loading up the Sperry ball turret. Armed with twin .50 calibre machine guns, the turret could rotate 360°; the guns could move 90° up or down. The ball turret gunner was the least popular role among B-17 crews since the gunner could easily be in position within the cramped space for five to six hours. The gunner would enter the turret mid-flight, manually cranking the turret until the guns were facing the tail and pointing down. In this position the entry hatch could be opened and a waist gunner would assist the gunner into position, lying on his back under the guns with his feet in stirrups. The vertical axis on the gun sight was controlled by his right foot; two handles located above his head contained the controls to rotate the turret, control the horizontal axis and fire the guns. In the event of an emergency, the gunner (wearing a chest chute) would open the hatch, unhook a safety belt and fall out.

B-17 ball turret gunner Staff Sergeant Donald Herman christened his turret Sadie's Baby. Clearly staged for the photograph, the aircraft manual cautioned: 'Do not attempt to rotate the turret in elevation while the airplane is on the ground. No crew member shall be in the turret during landing or take-off and the guns of the turret shall be in the horizontal position pointing aft.

Photographed from another bomber in formation, damaged B-17F 41-24406 *All American*, 97th BG, 414th BS, miraculously limps home to its base at Biskra, Algeria, on 1 February 1943.

During a bombing mission over Tunisia, a German Focke-Wulf Fw 190 fighter from II/JG 2 whose pilot had been killed, crashed into *All American*. The impact tore the fuselage open and severed the left horizontal stabiliser and elevator. Miraculously none of the crew were injured. Staff Sergeant Sam Sarpolus remained at his tail gun position until the last enemy fighter had gone. Afterwards he recalled that he felt 'like he was riding on the end of a kite, zig-zagging through space'. An hour and a half later, Pilot Lieutenant Kendrick R. Bragg Jr. brought the crippled craft home to a safe landing. Shortly after the incident, singer Eddie Cantor dedicated the song *Comin' in on a Wing and a Prayer* to Bragg and his crew. The song became a number one hit in 1943. According to Bombardier Ralph Burbridge, Boeing engineers later said, 'Because we got rammed in the air it was impossible to fly [*All American*] but we did. Ken was a good pilot and our co-pilot – Godfrey Murphy – was too. Co-pilots don't get very much attention but he was a very good pilot.'

Home safely. *All American*'s tail purportedly broke off while under examination by three ground personnel. Burbridge recalled 'how our ground crew had given us up so they were really glad to see us… Our crew chief, the head mechanic, had tears in his eyes.'

Close up view of the extensive tail damage. B-17 Navigator William T. White, B-17F 41-24412 *Flying Flint Gun*, was an observer to the incident, 'On one of our missions from Biskra to Bizerte, a German fighter, most likely out of control from B-17 hits, collided with one of the B-17s. The B-17 was virtually cut into two pieces, but somehow was held together by the catwalk/spine that ran the length of the plane. We flew alongside the plane until it made it back to Biskra. Upon landing, the plane buckled at its tear, but the crew was uninjured. The picture of that plane, which I believe was taken by our co-pilot [Lieutenant Charles Cutforth] or someone else on our crew, established the toughness reputation of the B-17 and became a major photograph of World War II.'

All American was repaired and transferred in early March 1943 to the 353rd BS, 301st BG at St. Donat, Algeria. This photograph was taken several months after the bomber's final combat mission. It is seen here as a utility aircraft minus all guns, gun turrets and armour.

B-17E *Sea Breeze*, 376th BG, 512th BS, undergoing repairs at Gura Air Depot, Eritrea, after service over Libya. Pilot Captain Earle A Goodrich was awarded the Silver Star for gallantry in action during a raid on Tobruk on 6 November 1942. 'Acting as Pilot, he showed such superb control over his craft that he kept in a good formation which not only completed a perfect bomb pattern but also presented a formidable front to the enemy aircraft, and was thereby a contributor to the success of the mission. The bombing run was made and anti-aircraft fire was intense and exceedingly accurate. As soon as the ground fire was out-distanced, the enemy fighters began to attack, but due to the perfect formation held by the bombers, the attacks were warded off with the shooting down of one plane and probable damage to others. The raid resulted in the confirmed sinking of a large enemy supply transport and the confirmed sinking of a medium Axis submarine. Without the skill of Lieutenant Goodrich, it is doubtful if that particular plane would have returned safely to its base.' In January 1943 Goodrich later made a belly landing in the desert in transit to Biskra, Algeria, where his aircraft was to join the 301st BG.

B-17G 42-31182 *The Mighty Rabbit* of the 301st BG, 419th BS. William T. White noted, 'Although our airplanes were frequently damaged by the strong defences at our targets, it soon became clear that our major maintenance and repair problem was not combat damage but desert sand. The planes' engines had worked well in rainy England, but did not have filters effective against the Sahara sand that was sucked into their cylinders on every take-off and landing at Biskra.' White recalled another incident at the airfield: 'One morning we were all ordered to a large field near our parked aircraft to witness the execution by a French firing squad of four saboteurs… Each of the condemned men was tied to a stake about half his height. I was later told that the bent-over position was used to facilitate the "coup de grace" mercy shot fired by the French officer in charge of the firing squad just in case the firing squad's bullets had not been fatal.'

B-17 flying officers congratulate intelligence officer Captain Gilbert B. Pearsall after he was awarded the Air Medal and Oak Leaf Clusters. Pearsall was one of the few ground officers to receive the medal. Combat veteran B-17F *Invictus* provides the backdrop.

Pilot Major Robert E. Kimmel and crew. A native of Mercer County, Ohio, Kimmel named his B-17 *Mercer County Special*. Recipient of the Silver Star and Distinguished Flying Cross, Kimmel remembered how the '*Special* was a good plane,' though 'I emerged without a scratch but the same cannot be said for her.' The bomber's demise occurred in February 1943, while Kimmel was temporarily assigned to another aircraft, when it was hit by gunfire on approach to a landing in Algeria. 'They patch up aircraft that are badly damaged but the *Mercer County Special* was too far gone for even the best of patching… Good parts were salvaged and the rest became junk.' In October 1943 Kimmel was selected to fly General Carl A. Spaatz, commander of US Air Forces in Africa, to Washington, D.C. Afterwards Spaatz selected Kimmel as his personal pilot – a post held until the general's retirement in 1948. 'Without the B-17,' wrote General Carl Spaatz, 'we might have lost the war.'

B-17F 41-24418 *Mickey Finn* was initially assigned to the 301st BG and flew eleven missions under that name. When the group was transferred to Tafaraoui, Algeria, the bomber was renamed *Special Delivery II* after *Special Delivery I* was scrapped due to flak damage. After completing a further sixty-eight missions, the war weary bomber returned to the US where it was used in a training role. It was written off in 1944.

Members of the 301st BG celebrate their 100th mission – a raid on Leghorn, Italy—having never lost a crewmember in combat. In the background is B-17F 42-5456 *Adele's Angel*.

General Buggies. Major General Lewis H. Brereton (right) and Major Max R. Fennell snapped before the latter's personal plane: B-17E 41-9029 *Fennell vs Rommel*, 7th BG.

Brigadier General James Doolittle prepares to take off in B-17 41-24576 *Peggy D II*, 97th BG, at a Moroccan airfield.

The crew of B-17F 41-24346 Avenger 301st BG, 419th BS, are interrogated after a raid on Naples on 4 April 1943 – the first raid on continental Europe by the Northwest African Air Force. The bomber returned to the US in 1944 where it was sold for scrap.

B-17F 41-24412 *Flying Flit Gun*, 301st BS, 97th BG at Maison Blanche airfield, Algiers. Margaret Bourke-White, the first accredited female US war photojournalist, was asked by one bomber's crew to name their plane. She chose *Flying Flit Gun* (a *Flit gun* is a hand-pumped insecticide sprayer), which was duly painted onto the nose beside a bug sprayer directed at three insects bearing the faces of Hitler, Mussolini and Hirohito. Bourke-White was delighted to see her nickname 'Peggy' adorning the No.3 engine, an honour usually reserved for wives and fiancées, when she christened the Flying Fortress with a bottle of Coke.

The Regensburg Raid

On 17 August 1943, Major General Ira C. Eaker, 8th Air Force, launched a combined raid – an audacious double strike to confuse German controllers and exhaust their fighter pilots – deep into the Third Reich. Colonel Curtis E. LeMay's force of 146 bombers struck the Regensburg Messerschmitt works in Bavaria before continuing onward to Tunisia; the remaining 230 aircraft under Brigadier General Robert B. Williams bombed the Schweinfurt ball-bearing factories and returned to England. Divisionary attacks were undertaken against Luftwaffe airfields and coastal targets. Approximately 300 waiting German fighters attacked LeMay's bombers, which were unescorted from the Belgian frontier, en route to their target. The local population, gazing skyward, assumed the US bombers, which were flying in (mutually-supporting) textbook formation in clear skies, were Luftwaffe aircraft since enemy daylight raids had never flown so deep into Germany before. Defence of the Messerschmitt factory complex fell to twelve pilots from the *Industrieschutzstaffel* (factory protection squadron) and flak. Nearly 300 tons of bombs were dropped from a height of 5-6,000 metres destroying 37 new aircraft and killing 400 people. The main target however, the vast assembly plant, was not hit and aircraft production was only temporarily interrupted. US bombs, however, did destroy the fuselage jigs for the new Me 262 jet fighter. Turning south and crossing the Swiss Alps, the embattled B-17s flew towards primitive North African airfields, which they reached after an average of eleven hours in the air. LeMay lost twenty-four B-17s: fourteen were shot down, two force-landed in Switzerland, four crashed in southern Europe and four ditched in the Mediterranean off Tunisia. Another fifty required repairs in North Africa.

A B-17 of the 385th BG lands Telergma Airfield, some 300 kilometres south of Algiers. Despite the loss of fifty-five bombers and 552 crewmen, the overall mission was judged a success. The BGs involved were awarded the Presidential Unit Citation.

Sheltering from the fierce African sun. B-17F 42-3290 *Raunchy Wolf*, 551st BS, 385th BG, and crew. This bomber was later involved in a mid-air collision with another B-17, 42-30264 *Dorsal Queen* near West Hordon, Essex, on 26 September 1943. A witness to the accident stated, 'Suddenly this B-17 appeared to go out of control and plunge vertically earthward. As it fell its wing tip struck the rear fuselage of a second B-17 between the mid-upper gunner and the fin completely severing the tail section including the rear gun turret complete with gunner. A large section of wing from the first B-17 also tore away. Both aircraft immediately began to fall, the B-17 minus its tail in a flat spin, the other in a steep spiral dive, no parachutes were observed.'

Airmen from B-17F 42-5913 *Shack Bunny*, 551st BS, 385th BG, and civilians (note the camel) at Telergma airfield, Algeria. The objective to fly from the European target onward to North Africa in an attempt to confuse German defenders and take advantage of the Mediterranean weather proved disappointing. Aside from the unavailability of maintenance crews upon landing, the journey to distant North Africa placed a heavy strain on flight crews. This raid was the first of several 8th Air Force shuttle missions in which the participating bombers would land at several different airfields and later bomb a second target on the return flight home.

B-17F *Shack Bunny* and crew. 'We had the greatest time in North Africa,' a crewmember of another B-17 wrote to his mother. 'The greatest treat of all was that we got all the fresh eggs, vegetables and fresh fruit that we could eat. Also white bread (French), which is unheard of in England. For a week we just laid around in the nice warm sun and swam and ate and went to town.'

The smiling crew of *Shack Bunny* enjoy some shade under their B-17's wing. Regensburg was costly — nearly 40 per cent of LeMay's bombers were either shot down or reached North Africa with enough damage to ground them. Sixty B-17s were left behind on the return journey several days later that included a 'milk run' raid over Bordeaux, France. *Shack Bunny* was later lost over France on 20 October 1943 during a raid against Düren, Germany. The crew were taken prisoner.

A B-17 co-pilot from the 95th BG wrote, 'After fighting in the skies all day — eleven hours and twenty minutes of recorded flight time with about three of it under the fiercest of all fighter attacks — our crew arrived in North Africa.' A bed was made 'on the wing of the airplane. It is hard; not level, and there is the possibility of falling the ten or twelve feet to the ground. We are so tired, however, we have no trouble sleeping.' Note the formation lights below the B-17's rear twin guns, the tail-wheel gear, and the 26-inch smooth contour tyre that retracted into into the aft section of the waist gun compartment after take-off.

Having survived Regensburg, B-17F 42-30278 *Sly Fox*, 385th BG, was damaged in a taxiing accident seven days later. Flying Fortresses on this mission were specially equipped with so-called 'Tokyo tanks' to provide the extra range needed to strike the target and continue onward to North Africa.

Sly Fox's tail fin was severed when it came off the steel runway matting and collided with another B-17. The damage was successfully repaired and the Fortress returned to England where it joined the 418th BS, 100th BG.

An unusual 'souvenir' from North Africa. 'Many of the GIs,' recalled a 95th BG crewman, 'made deals with the local Arabs [at Bône airfield, Algeria] for trinkets and clothing, but two guys from squadron traded for a miniature donkey. It was dark brown and had big ears. How they thought they'd be able to sneak it on board a B-17, I don't know. The legend has it that they wrapped her in a blanket and slipped back to their tent. When it was time to depart, they shoved the little donkey through the hatch and into the waist. "Little Mo" quieted down while the plane took off and headed back to England… The two gunners and the donkey shared their oxygen all the way home.' Pilot Harry M. Conley remembered 'looking out the window at that plane and I could see the donkey with an oxygen mask over his snout. His large ears were quite visible.' The donkey survived the journey back to Horham, Suffolk, where donkey cart rides were given to the local children. Unfortunately Little Mo succumbed to the English weather during the winter of 1943-44. The poor animal's final 'mission' was being dropped complete with dog tags and surplus uniform near the initial point on a bombing mission. 'Unfortunately no one can record the confusion and consternation of the German people assigned to grave registration,' commented pilot 1st Lieutenant John A. Storie of B-17F 42-29694 *Southern Belle*.

B-17F 42-30246 *Spot Remover* 570BS/390BG aircrew and locals. The bomber later crash-landed on 20 February 1944 near Tirstrup, Denmark, after running low on fuel following a raid on Rostock, Germany.

A long way from home – another 385th BG B-17 in North Africa.

B-17 42-29480 *Cotton Eyed Joe* B-17 42-29480 after belling landing at Tafaraoui, Algeria. A contemporary rhyme described the mud as 'deep and gooey'.

1st Lieutenant Joseph A. Archambault stands before B-17 42-29480 *Cotton Eyed Joe*.

B-17F 42-5776 *Eager Beaver* of the 2nd BG, 96th BS. Note the cheek gun mounting, an installation found only in Lockheed-Vega built B-17Fs. This veteran of twenty-six missions (when this photograph was taken) was later hit by flak over Aloysius Airfield, Athens, and crashed on 20 December 1943. Tail gunner John Carson recalled: 'The Aloysius mission was supposed to be an easy target. It turned out to be anything but. As we approached the target, heavy and extremely accurate 88-mm flak started to rise, and we took some bad licks. We were lead plane at an altitude of 21,500 feet approaching the indicated point (IP), the point where the bombardier takes control of the plane. Since the bombardier needs a steady plane to aim the bomb drop, no evasive manoeuvres can be made from the IP until the bombs are away. As we approached the IP, the flak grew heavier. Just as we made the IP, all hell broke loose…we had taken a severe hit under the aircraft…another 88 burst over and straight behind the vertical stabiliser, just aft of the plane… A third flak burst had struck us at the waist door, severing the entire tail from the rest of the plane.' Incredibly, five airmen survived.

Blowout. Engineers assess the damage to a shredded tyre after a Fortress' landing gear was damaged by flak during a raid on Naples Harbour, 4 April 1943. One aircraft MIA that day was the B-24D Liberator *Lady Be Good* from the 514th BS, 376th BG. After all attempts to locate the plane had failed, the aircrew were classified as missing in action, presumed dead. Only later in November 1958 was the wreckage found deep in the Libyan desert. Two years later the bodies of eight airmen who had bailed out were found; the body of the radio operator was never found.

Staff Sergeant Richard W. Dunlap poses before B-17F 42-29513 *El Diablo*, 346th BS, 99th BG. *El Diablo* completed 114 missions with the 99th BG. Colonel Fay R. Upthegrove, group commanding officer, later used the aircraft as his personal transport. Upthegrove's military career spanned three decades, including service in the Far East, African, and European theatres of operation. After leaving the 99th BG in November of 1943, Upthegrove became commander of the 304th Bomb Wing, 15th Air Force, in Italy.

Engine maintenance on B-17F 42-5346, *The Reluctant Dragon*. Manufactured by Hamilton Standard, the three bladed B-17 propellers were hydromatic controlled, full feathering. They measured 11 feet 7 inches in diameter.

According to the B-17 pilot's manual: 'The Wright model R-1820-97 Cyclone 9 engines are air-cooled, nine-cylinder radial aircraft engines, equipped with integral reduction gears through which the propellers are driven. A type B-2 General Electric turbosupercharger is provided for each engine to boost manifold pressure for take-off and high-altitude flight… Should engine control cables be shot away, four of the controls will automatically assume predetermined positions: throttles, wide open; superchargers, 65 per cent power; intercoolers, cold; and propellers, 1850 rpm.'

Re-fitting the tail of B-17 42-5346 *The Reluctant Dragon*, flown by Captain Marion Jones of the 414th BS, 97th BG, in Algiers, 1943. In a contemporary magazine advertisement, Boeing boasted that 'Despite the many difficulties entailed in the building of so complicated a weapon, Boeing is able to hatch out Flying Fortresses in constantly accelerated volume, because it has reduced even the most involved procedures to simple, accurate operations which can be quickly learned by men or women without previous mechanical experience. This means manufacturing planning of the highest order. Each part, each function, each assembly (and they total thousands) had to be arranged and tooled. Boeing, for example, developed more than 100,000 *special* tools to do the job.'

The Flying Fortress was renowned for absorbing combat damage. Here 2nd Lieutenant Orlof Duker points to the flak-damaged rudder of B-17 42-3189 *The Red Ass* (*Superstitious Aloysius*) 99th BG, 347th BS. A wartime technical document explained that the 'dorsal fin, while part of the vertical tail surfaces, acts to carry a portion of the fin load forward to the fuselage structure, and at the same time is valuable in providing directional stability for the airplane. Structurally, the fin consists of hydropressed ribs and extruded stiffeners covered with 24-ST clad skin. The vertical stabiliser is similar in construction to the horizontal stabiliser. It is of two spar, web type, and formed of 24-ST extrusions for spar chords. Spanwise stiffeners are rolled 24-ST, and ribs are hydropress stampings of 24-ST sheet stock.'

Servicing B-17F 42-5772, 352nd BS, 301st BG outdoors at Marrakesh airfield, June 1943. Marrakesh Menara Airport operates today as an international Moroccan airport.

B-17s are serviced on an Algiers airfield by ground crewmen. B-17F 42-5346 *The Reluctant Dragon* appears again on the right.

Damaged B17s at Biskra are stripped for parts. Left: B-17F 41-24442 *Little Eva* 342nd BS, 97th BG was damaged by a Luftwaffe raid on 20 December 1942. Right: B-17F 41-24369 *Special Delivery* (originally slated for the RAF, serial FA684) 32nd BS/301st BG was hit by flak over Bizerte and crash-landed. Before the war, basic aircraft mechanic training was general in character. It was not until late 1942 that US technical schools began to provide specific maintenance instructions for individual aircraft.

Maison Blanche, Algiers. B-17F 41-24376 *Hellzapoppin* (originally assigned to the RAF) 341st BS, 97th BG, is ablaze after the airfield was bombed by nineteen Ju 88s from KG 64 on the night of 20/21 November 1942. The bomber was taxiing at the time of the attack; the crew were killed. One P-38 was also destroyed and three damaged. The German bombers also dropped four-pointed steel spikes that could puncture aircraft tyres.

The burnt-out remains of B-17 41-24376 *Hellzapoppin*.

Scrapped B17s are stripped of valuable parts to keep other Fortresses operational.

The outer skin of a derelict Flying Fortress is removed, revealing the bomber's internal framework. B-17F 41-24369 *Special Delivery*, originally assigned to the RAF (note the serial number FA 684 and over-painted roundel), was scrapped following flak damage during a mission to Bizerte and the subsequent crash landing at Maison Blanche.

Men from the 92nd Bomb Group at Algiers stand to attention while Lieutenant Colonel Elliott Roosevelt (son of Franklin D. Roosevelt) is presented with the Distinguished Flying Cross for 'heroism and extraordinary achievement' before and during the Torch landings. The closest aircraft behind the personnel, B-17E 41-9045 *Stinky*, was later lost in the war due to a (non-fatal) forced landing in Ireland on 15 January 1943. Photograph taken on 27 December 1942.

The Consolidated B-24 Liberator

The Consolidated B-24 was designed in response to a US Army Air Corps demand in early 1939. The heavy bomber featured an innovative high 'shoulder mounted' wing, twin vertical fin and rudders, and tricycle undercarriage. The flight crew comprised two pilots, bombardier, navigator, flight engineer, radio operator and four gunners. The aircraft was 66 feet 4 inches (20.2 metres) in length with a wingspan of 110 feet (33.5 metres) and an overall height of 17 feet 11 inches (5.5 metres). The Liberator had an empty weight of 32,605 pounds (14.8 tons) and a maximum take-off weight of 64,000 pounds (29 tons).

B-24D 41-11593 *Black Mariah II* was one of the original Halverson Project (HALPRO) aircraft, earmarked for an attack on mainland Japan from China before it was assigned to the 513th BS, 376th BG and transferred to North Africa. The B-24 pilot's manual highlighted the importance of his leadership: 'Your crew is made of up of specialists. Each man – whether his is the navigator, bombardier, engineer, or radio operator – is an expert in his line. But how well he does his job, and how efficiently he plays his part as a member of your combat team, will depend to a great extent on how well you play your own part as the airplane commander.'

Like the B-17, the B-24 was rugged and heavily armed. It was designed around the Davis high aspect ratio wing, an advanced airfoil that was 20 per cent more efficient than contemporary designs. Although the B-24 flew faster, further, and could carry a heavier payload compared with the B-17, it was not as reliable as the more famous Boeing aircraft. Fifteenth Air Force engineer 1st Lieutenant Bud Markel described the bomber as a 'cantankerous, lumbering, draughty, unforgiving son-of-a-bitch, heavy on the controls, overgrossed and difficult to fly in formation, with an ancient boiler-style fuel gauge system that was almost useless. The heaters never worked when you needed them, and were removed by many combat groups as being too dangerous to operate because of the fuel lines on the flight deck necessary to feed them.'

Closely parked B-24s. Upon his arrival at an Egyptian airfield on 13 July 1942, Lieutenant General Lewis H. Brereton noted in his diary: 'Came to the advance base here to observe the take-off of our heavies for tonight's mission. On arrival found nine heavies parked wing-tip to wing-tip on one runway, with a British Liberator squadron similarly parked. I stopped the briefing and gave instructions for the aircraft to be dispersed immediately.'

B-24 Pilot 1st Lieutenant Guyon Phillips recalled the handling aspects of the bomber. 'The Lib[erator] had great engines which gave you minimum problems. And it had the high-lift low-drag Davis wing (although the wing couldn't take the much damage compared to the Flying Fort[ress]. On the flip side, you could never trim the son-of-a-gun, and had to horse it around constantly. Flying formation gave your left arm a tremendous workout... You made no sudden moves in a B-24. Response time had to be calculated. And then there were the constant gas fumes... You always sweated out ditching when you were over open water. The high wing and the soft underbelly didn't offer you much chance if you had to down in the ocean.' With regard to the bomber's outward appearance compared to the B-17, another B-24 pilot commented that the bomber 'lacked the grace and beauty, especially when on the ground – where most people first glimpsed it.' The B-24's most distinctive feature was its twin-tail construction. In 1942 the army felt that a single-tail would provide greater stability, leading Consolidated to investigate changes. Test models were subsequently flown in 1943 with the Navy receiving the redesigned Liberator, which was dubbed the Consolidated PB4Y-2 Privateer.

B-24 captain and co-pilot—Captain J.W. Wilkinson (left), 1st Lieutenant J.R. Wilcox (right). The B-24D pilot's manual instructed: 'First and foremost importance, you are the Pilot; the lives of your crew and successful completion of your mission is in your hands. Use good judgement and common sense. The airplane is a piece of machinery and will react exactly as you direct. It will not fight back nor argue with you, so do not get mad at it, it only affects your own reactions and corresponding ability to fly... The B-24 airplane is not difficult to fly. It has no vicious characteristics and when the Pilot learns the difference in "feel", due to its size, weight, and speed range, flying it is no more of a problem than flying a trainer. A large bomber is a highly complicated piece of equipment containing many components. Learn your airplane, study the functional operations of the several systems and the mystery of imagined complexities will become surprisingly simple. A little time devoted to the fundamentals of what makes it "tick" will pay amazing dividends in psychological reaction and peace of mind. Master the airplane, don't let it master you, but – never lose respect for it.'

Waist gunner and radio operator/gunner. Pilots were taught there 'is a lot of radio equipment in today's B-24s. There is one special man who is supposed to know all there is to know about this equipment. Sometimes he does but often he doesn't. His deficiencies often do not become apparent until the crew is in the combat zone, when it is too late. Too often the lives of pilots and crew are lost because the radio operator has accepted his responsibility indifferently. Radio is a subject that cannot be learned in a day. It cannot be mastered in six weeks, but sufficient knowledge can be imparted to the radio man during his period of training in the United States providing he is willing to study.' Pictured on the ground in shirts with sleeves rolled up, a former 15th AAF gunner explained the hardship that was exposure to the cold: 'Flying between 20,000 and 25,000 feet altitude the temperature could reach between 40 to 60 degrees below zero. Protected only by an electrically heated suit (jacket, trousers, gloves and boots), it was sometimes difficult to keep warm, especially in the waist section with open waist windows.' 'Bone chilling cold was the constant companion of every Liberator crew member,' recalled another B-24 veteran. An additional problem for waist position crew was the absence of seats and restraints, despite the numerous sharp objects that often inflicted severe injuries on unrestrained crew during a collision, forced-landing, ditching or even in the event of severe turbulence.

B-24 waist gunner. The waist gunner positions on later model aircraft were staggered to reduce the likelihood of adjacent gunners bumping each other. The abovementioned manual asked: 'Are you ready to fight? Are your guns working? The only way you can be sure is to know how competent and reliable your gunners are. It is uncomfortable to get caught by a swarm of enemy fighters and find that your guns won't function... While the flexible gunner does not require the same delicate touch as the turret gunner, he must have a fine sense of timing and be familiar with the rudiments of exterior ballistics.'

Homing pigeons are handed to a B-24 crewmember, pre-flight, during the summer of 1943. The birds were trained by RAF personnel attached to the 376th BG, based near Benghasi, Libya. Every bomber carried two birds on a combat mission. The recommended way to release a pigeon mid-flight was to place it in a paper sack and drop it out of the waist window. Although the scheme extended over several months there are no recorded situations in which the birds were used in an emergency.

Operation Tidal Wave

Low flying B-24s practice for Operation Tidal Wave – a daring low-level attack on the nine oil refineries in the Romanian city of Ploesti. Within a month of Pearl Harbor, US planners had begun studying the feasibility of a raid against Ploesti to deny the Axis petroleum-based fuel as part of an 'oil campaign'. An earlier mission by thirteen HALPRO B-24s, the first USAAF bombing mission against a European target, had bombed the Astra Romana refinery on 12 June 1942. Although actual damage was negligible, the mission alerted the Luftwaffe to the likelihood of future raids (the Russians had already bombed the oilfields in the summer of 1941 and again in September 1942 with limited success).

The Allies agreed at the Casablanca Conference in January 1943 to undertake a major daylight raid against Ploesti. Initially codenamed *Operation Soapsuds*, Winston Churchill intervened, criticising the name as 'inappropriate for an operation in which so many brave Americans would risk or lose their lives... I do not think it is good for morale to affix disparaging labels to daring feats of arms'. The operation was accordingly renamed *Tidal Wave*. Since Ploesti was beyond the range of bombers based in England, the mission was assigned to US 9th Air Force B-24s based in North Africa. The plan involved a force of 178 B-24s and 1,751 airmen flying from Libya and before dividing in two groups – the 376th and 93rd BGs led by Colonel Keith K. Compton; the 44th, 98th and 389th BGs led by Colonel John R. Kane. The raid was planned for Sunday, 1 August 1943.

The operation began on an inauspicious note. One bomber crashed on take-off. The lead aircraft, B-24D 42-40563 *Wongo Wongo*, inexplicably crashed into the Mediterranean; another broke protocol to investigate and was unable to re-join the force. A further ten bombers were forced to abort due to mechanical issues, reducing the attacking force to 165 aircraft. Despite radio silence, German intelligence intercepted an informal message announcing the departure of the bombers from Benghazi and placed their forces on alert. Radar also tracked the US aircraft as they crossed the Mediterranean. Swinging northeast across Albania and Yugoslavia, the already drawn-out force grew even farther apart. Nearing a mountain range engulfed by heavy cloud cover, four group commanders chose to fly over the clouds while another – Colonel John R. Kane's 98th BG – went under, placing the group further behind and further mixing up the attack sequence. A fatal navigational error by Colonel Keith Compton (376th BG) in the lead new plane *Teggie Ann* (carrying Brigadier General Uzal G. Ent) then brought the force on a course towards Bucharest instead of Ploesti. Dozens of aircrew broke radio silence to yell 'mistake' or 'not here!'. Correcting their approach, the US bombers closed on their target through skies filled with flak, barrage balloons and waiting fighter aircraft. Amidst the confusion, different aircraft formations approached Ploesti at low level from different directions. Pilots battled to avoid collisions amidst sheets of flame from exploding bombs. Turning for home, waves of battered B-24s were picked off by Bulgarian and German fighter aircraft. Only eighty-eight bombers returned to Benghazi, fifty-five with combat damage. Damage to the refineries was soon repaired.

The 15th Air Force returned to Ploesti in 1944 during twenty-four strikes and 5,675 sorties, but Tidal Wave stands as the only low-level heavy US bomber mission of the war. Fuel production at Ploesti had virtually ended by the time Romania switched sides in August 1944.

A ground crew member of the 376th Bomb Group 'Liberandos' polishes the Plexiglas nose of B-24D 41-23724 *Doodlebug*, 512th BS, 376th BG. Looking on is a solemn William G. Jordan, the bomber's radio operator/waist gunner. This aircraft was originally assigned to the 93rd BG, 8th Air Force, before it was badly damaged in a crash landing due to combat damage on 15 January 1943. Once repaired it was transferred to the 512th BS, 376th BG. The combat veteran ended its days as a 449th BG transport.

General Brereton's assessment of the low-level Ploesti mission was glum: 'We expect our losses to be fifty percent but even if we lose everything we've sent but hit the target, it will be worth it.' Nevertheless, motivation was high among the aircrew: 'If you knock it out the way you should, it will probably shorten the war… If you do your job right, it is worth it, even if you lose every plane.' Note that the Norden bombsights were removed from the aircraft before the mission and replaced by rudimentary aiming devices. Two auxiliary bomb-bay fuel tanks were also installed, giving a capacity of 3,100 gallons.

Staff Sergeant Joseph E. Tamuleirz (gunner) passes a flak jacket through the waist window to *Doodlebug*'s radio operator/waist gunner, William G. Jordan.

The use of body armour in aircraft was based on a study of wound ballistics by U.S. Colonel Malcolm. C. Grow. Two types of armour were developed by Wilkinson Sword using Du Pont's ballistic nylon. Both could stop shrapnel but not bullets.

1st Lt John E. McAtee, pilot of B-24D 41-23724 *Doodlebug* prepares for Tidal Wave. Awakened by 0400, the aircrew received a hurried breakfast before taking off by 0730.

Pilots and crew of *Doodlebug*. Standing L-R SGT Robert T. Butler, gunner, S/SGT Joseph E. Tamueircz, waist gunner, S/SGT Libert T. Hurt, waist gunner, T/SGT Kenneth W. Smith, flight engineer/top turret, T/SGT William G. Jordan, radio operator, S/SGT Murray L. Heckert, tail gunner. Seated L-R 2nd Lt Robert J. Johnson, navigator, 2nd Lt Israel Soloff, bombardier, 1st Lt James W. Welch, Jr, co-pilot, 1st Lt John E. McAtee, pilot.

The crew of B-24D 42-40664 *Teggie Ann* (formerly *Honey Chile*) arrive in preparation for the Ploesti raid. The two meals served to the aircrew before the mission, steak flown in from Cairo and a breakfast of real eggs (not powdered), had the opposite effect to their intended morale boost. For many men, it felt as if they were on death row. Both Britain's Air Chief Marshal Sir Arthur Tedder and General Dwight D. Eisenhower had urged Brereton to cancel the mission.

Teggie Ann's flight engineer and three gunners don their newly issued flak jackets. A waist gunner from the 351st BG described wearing the protective jacket: 'The flak suit consisted of four aprons of two-inch platelets, overlapping like fish scales. Two of the aprons were for the front and two for the back. The flak jacket fastened at the shoulder with four snaps and had an emergency release where, if needed, you could pull a strap and they'd fall off. The top half of the apron would cover the chest and the bottom, the thighs and crotch. They weighed between fifteen and twenty pounds. They were not bullet proof but would stop low-velocity projectiles such as flak shrapnel or pistol bullets. They'd been known to help men to survive 20-mm shell hits.'

Colonel Keith K. Compton (centre), commanding officer of the 376th BG, and Brigadier General Uzal G. Ent (right) commander of 9th Bomber Command, pictured in front of B-24D *Teggie Ann*, the lead aircraft on the Ploesti raid.

Lt. Gen. Lewis Brereton originally intended to lead the mission until overruled by General Henry Arnold. Brereton was simply too valuable to risk falling into enemy hands. The next senior ranking officer who could participate was Brigadier General Uzal G. Ent, seen with pilot Col. Keith K. Compton beside B-24D *Teggie Ann* just before take-off.

The B-24 crews had practiced missions against a dummy target, a reproduction of the Ploesti targets, in a remote area of the desert. It was bombed repeatedly until, as one crew member penned, 'we could bomb it in our sleep.' The actual mission was armed 1000-pound and 500-pound demolition bombs, totalling 310 tons, plus 290 boxes of British-type and 140 clusters of US-type incendiaries.

Six hours after leaving Benghazi, Ent radioed 'Mission successful' to Brereton. The large number of distress calls picked up by the RAF, however, presented a different story as surviving aircraft struggled to return home.

Technical Sergeant A. Trozzi and Corporal Peter Holko roll a 500-pound bomb along in preparation for the Ploesti raid. A combination of ten-second delay fused and twenty-minute acid core fused bombs were dropped. B-24D 41-11636 *Wash's Tub*, 514th BS, 376th BG, a HALPRO raid veteran, survived to return to the US in September 1943 for a War Bond tour. The Liberator saw use as a training aircraft before being scrapped in October 1944. During its fifteen months in the Middle East, 41-11636 flew seventy-three missions, dropped 219 tons of bombs and shot down twenty-two fighters. Note the yellow edge around the aircraft's national insignia.

B-24D *Teggie Ann* pictured taxiing at Benina airfield, Libya. This aircraft was later shot down on a raid on 16 August 1943 by Unteroffizier Martin Muller flying Bf 109G-6 of JG 3/12 while on a mission to bomb Foggia, Italy.

Lewis N. Ellis, pilot of B-24D 41-11815 *Daisy Mae* later wrote, 'Altogether the [Ploesti] briefing was comparatively short for so important a mission, but practically everything had already been covered many times in previous sessions… Take off was scheduled for 6.30 A.M… As we taxied out, everyone was surprisingly quiet and confident, at least outwardly. During our few missions in Africa we had learned something about fear and how to control it.' Each B-24 carried approximately 3,100 gallons of fuel plus an average load of 4,300 pounds of bombs and bullets, which exceeded the bomber's maximum load capability and made take off a major undertaking.'

B-24D 42-40364 *Snow White and the Seven Dwarfs* of 98th BG 'Pyramiders' was shot down by Bf-109 fighters from JG-27 over Bulgaria. Tail gunner Stanley M. Horine, the sole survivor, spent the remainder of the war as a POW. (Amos Nicholson, Crew Chief of the 343rd BS, 98th BG, painted the nose art)

B-24D 41-11630 *Kitty Quick* (earlier known as *Chum V*) 515th BS, 376th BG, survived the raid and returned to Libya.

376th BG B-24s before the raid. Operation Tidal Wave was undertaken from five temporary desert bases scattered around Benghazi, Libya. Closest to the camera is B-24D 41-24294 *Brewery Wagon*, which broke formation over target. Flying alone, it was hit by flak before a German Bf 109 delivered the *coup de grâce*. Next in line are B-24D 41-24258 *Desert Lilly* and B-24D 42-40563 *Wongo Wongo*. The latter inexplicably stood on its tail in mid-air before spinning out of formation and crashing into the Mediterranean off Corfu en route to the target. The pilot of *Desert Lily* then broke procedure and formation to circle the wreckage in vain. Unable to catch up with the rest of the formation, the bomber was left behind and forced to abort the mission. *Desert Lily* was later shot down by a Bf 109G-6 near Wiemath, Austria, on 2 November 1943.

B-24D 41-11819, 344th BS, 98th BG *Raunchy* was shot down near the target. Eight crew were killed and two taken prisoner.

Colonel Jacob E. Smart, the architect of the Ploesti plan, recognised the shortcomings of the B-24 for the mission: its relatively small bomb load plus its big, box-car-like configuration was ill-suited for a low level mission.

B-24D 42-40563 *Wongo Wongo*, the lead ship with Lieutenant Robert F. Wilson the mission navigator crashed into the Mediterranean en route to Ploesti. An observer in B-24D 41-24032 *Let's Go* noted the time – 0822. The incident caused much confusion in the formation, especially in view of radio silence.

Piloted by Lieutenant Donaldson B. Hurd, B-24D 42-40319 *Dopey Goldberg*, renamed *Yankee Rebel*, 515th BS, 376th BG, 9th AF, returned safely to Libya.

The retraction speeds of the B-24's two main undercarriage gears were not synchronised, meaning one wheel would retract after the other, a feature that gave the unusual looking bomber a crippled appearance.

Low level flight over the Mediterranean Sea toward the Ploesti oil refineries in Romania. The closest aircraft to the camera is B-24D 42-72772 of the 376th BG. Note the gunner standing in the waist position.

Low flying B-24 *Daisy Mae* photographed from an even lower flying bomber. Captain Philip Ardery, 389th BG, wrote of 'More explosions and higher flames. Already the fires were leaping higher than the level of our approach. We had gauged ourselves to clear the tallest chimney in the plant by a few feet. Now there was a mass of flame and black smoke reaching much higher, and there were intermittent explosions lighting up the black pall.' Colonel Leon Johnson, 44th BG, described how 'we flew through sheets of flame, and airplanes were everywhere, some of them on fire and others exploding. It's indescribable to anyone who wasn't there.'

Lieutenant Robert Sternfels battles to pilot B-24D 42-40402, *The Sandman*, over target, buffeted by exploding bombs dropped by an earlier wave. *The Sandman* was shot down over northern Italy on 19 December 1943. Not until October 2001 was the wreckage discovered in the Dolomite Mountains. The aircrew's remains were returned to the US and buried in St. Louis, Missouri.

Anxious ground crew scan the sky for aircraft returning from Tidal Wave, an operation afterwards remembered as Black Sunday. Only eighty-eight B-24s returned to Libya, including fifty-four with combat damage too serious for them to ever fly in combat again. The final aircraft to land was B-24D 41-23742 *Liberty Lad*, which touched down sixteen hours after taking off with two engines out on one wing, no hydraulics, brakes or instrument lighting.

The tallest man in the 9th AF heavy bomb group, 2nd Lieutenant Carl S. Looker, pictured with 2nd Lieutenant Edward Rothkrug, in front of B-24D 41-11921 *Northern Star*, 343rd BS, 98th BG. *Northern Star* returned safely despite being intercepted by enemy fighters over Bulgaria. Looker, who piloted the B-24 41-11767 *Shanghi-Lil*, aborted the mission before reaching the objective.

1st Lieutenant Dean E. Lear, pilot of B-24D 42-40660 *Little Richard*, 513th BS, 376th BG, atttends a mission debrief. 'Chaos,' according to one account, 'clearly reigned in the skies over Ploesti. Bombers attacked the refineries from all sides, criss-crossing the oilfields in an attempt to find their designated targets, but at low levels, at speeds of 200 mph and distracted by flak, navigation was extremely difficult. Some refineries were not bombed at all; others were bombed twice. Most of the bombers ranged over the general Ploesti target area and unloaded on anything that looked good.' US intelligence grossly underestimated the Ploesti defences and losses were high. Figures vary, but it is commonly accepted that fifty-four aircraft were lost in combat, eight landed in neutral Turkey while nineteen limped home to make emergency landings at Cyprus, Malta and Sicily. Three bombers crashed at sea. A total of 310 aircrew were killed, 108 were taken prisoner by Axis forces, and another seventy-eight were interned in Turkey. Another four men listed as MIA were helped by Tito's partisans in Yugoslavia. Altogether 532 men were either dead, taken prisoner, missing or interned from a total of 1,726 who took part in the operation.

Cairo, 3 September 1943. Colonel Keith K. Compton is awarded a cluster to his DFC by Lieutenant General Lewis Brereton. Every Tidal Wave participant received the DFC. Wrote Brereton, 'My last official act as commander of the Ninth Air Force in the Middle East was to award decorations for Ploesti in an impressive ceremony attended by representatives of the British and Egyptian forces, as well as over 2,000 Americans, on the polo field of the swank Gezira Sporting Club... In all, five Congressional Medals of Honor were awarded for the Ploesti raid [three posthumously], the highest number ever given for any single military operation in our country's history.' But what of the damage caused? One of the nine refineries (a modern aviation fuel plant) was out of operation for the remainder of the war; two were not bombed at all, and the remaining refineries were largely repaired within a matter of weeks with the aid of 10,000 forced laborers. Idle plants were reactivated and production soon exceeded pre-raid levels. Given the loss of life and aircraft and relatively limited damage, the operation is considered a strategic failure, remembered today more for the valour of the aircrew involved. Eisenhower judged the raid as 'reasonably successful' and summed up the effort: 'As usual, mathematical calculations could not win over unexpected conditions.'

Office of War Information (OWI) photographer Nick Parrino: 'B-24 bombers of the 9th Air Force, somewhere in Libya, 1943'.

Yugoslav B24s

King Peter II of Yugoslavia is shown the controls of a Consolidated B-24. In September 1943 Washington donated four B-24 bombers to the king and the Royal Yugoslav government, based in exile in Cairo. At an earlier dedication ceremony, President Roosevelt declared, 'May these planes fulfil their mission…with two great objectives. The first is to drop bombs on our common enemy successfully and at the right points. The second is to deliver to your compatriots in Yugoslavia the much needed supplies for which they have waited so long – food, medicine – yes, arms and ammunition.' The king, in turn, cabled Roosevelt on 2 November to express his gratitude for the 'truly magnificent machines', adding, 'I take this opportunity to renew my personal and my people's warmest thanks to you Mr President, and to the American nation for this generous gift.'

After training in the US, the Yugoslav airmen flew their aircraft to Cairo where the king officially accepted the bombers at John H. Payne Field (named in honour of Lieutenant Colonel John H. Payne, 376th BG, KIA over enemy territory on 11 January 1943). The four aircraft were attached to the 376th BG, based at Enfidaville, Tunisia. Their first mission was against Eleusis Airport, Athens, on 15 November 1943. Of the four aircraft, three were shot down: B-24 42-73137 on 24 November 1943 over Sofia, Bulgaria; 42-73089 on 19 December 1943 over Augsburg, Germany; and 42-73085 on 22 August 1944 after a raid on Lobau, Austria. Only the bomber closest to the camera, B-24 42-73065, survived. The aircraft are seen with both US and Yugoslav insignia.

A Yugoslavian bomber crew pictured in front of their B-24J. While intended for propaganda purposes, the US ambassador to the Yugoslav government was cautioned to avoid 'further gifts of this character', lest it irritate Tito and the PLA (Peoples Liberation Army) – one of the 'bravest and most effective fighting groups in occupied Europe'.

Homeward bound. B-24D Liberator 41-11636 *Wash's Tub*, one of the 'Liberandos', 514th BS, 376th BG, was originally HALPRO aircraft No. 24 before being transferred to 98th BG and then to 376th. During its fifteen months of service in the Middle East, the bomber dropped 219 tons of bombs during 73 missions, spent 551 hours in combat and shot down 22 enemy fighters. The bomber returned to the US in September 1943 for a War Bond tour. Subsequently used as a training aircraft, it was scrapped in 1946. Standing L to R: Capt. Edward G. Feeley, Capt. Richard W. Beck, 1st Lt. Clifford R. Gugenhein, 1st Lt. Irving C. Bloom, T/Sgt Charles J. Cannon. Front L to R: S/Sgt Fred R. Bond, M/Sgt Richard C. Herbert, S/Sgt Ray W. Romick, T/Sgt Frederick P. Russek.

Pilot Lieutenant Royden L. Lebrecht admires the newly repainted artwork of B-24D 41-11761, *The Squaw*, 343rd BS, 98th BG. A veteran of the Ploesti raid, the bomber returned to the US for a War Bond Tour. The original nose art on the bomber was far cruder in both content and depiction.

The Squaw carried a tribute to the notable number of decorations awarded to 98th BG personnel on its aft fuselage. Some sources report that the bomber became a war memorial at Tampa Bay, Florida; others report that it was scrapped in November 1944.

In total, *The Squaw* dropped 360,000 pounds of bombs in Africa, Sicily, Greece, Crete and Rumania, completed 71 missions and downed 6 enemy planes. Standing L to R: Brig. Gen. Hoyt S. Vandenberg, Capt. Royden L. Lebrecht, 1st Lt. Clinton H. Killian, 1st Lt Albert J. Mickish, 1st Lt. Grover A. Zink, Lt. Robert H. Parham, T/Sgt John R. Reilly. Front L to R: T/Sgt Harold F. Weir, S/Sgt Paul E. Davidson, S/Sgt John A. Givens, S/Sgt Paul T. Baskis, S/Sgt John Gunnu, S/Sgt Adney J. Harmon.

USO entertainer Jack Benny christens the B-24D Liberator 41-24112 *Bucksheesh Benny Rides Again*, 389th BG, 566th BS as Larry Adler and army nurses look on. August 1943, Libya. The bomber later crash-landed in Egypt on 4 November 1943.

B-24D 42-40320 *Lucy's Lucky 13* belonged to the 98th BG, 345th BS. Curiously the number 13 has been painted over. The aircraft was later renamed *Wing and a Prayer*.

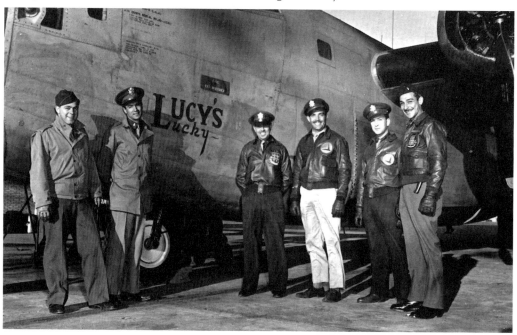

B-24D 41-11614 *Ripper the 1st*, 515th BS, 376th BG, suffered a nose-wheel failure after returning from the first US bombing raid on Rome. According to one Liberator pilot: 'Nose steering, such as today's power steering, was non-existent. Headway was maintained by throttles and brakes. The famously weak nose gear had a mind of its own, often collapsing of its own volition. So the flight engineer would have to sit astride the mechanism, waiting with a heavy foot to kick the stubborn thing down to lock.' The problem was caused by faulty actuating cylinders that raised and lowered the landing gear. In the 'down' position the cylinder became a stress-bearing member and the bolts used to fasten the ends of the cylinder to the gear and aircraft failed. Replacing the bolts with stronger case-hardened solid-shank eyebolts solved the problem.

Ripper the 1st photographed at Deversoir, Egypt, before the flight back to the US. As seen here, the elliptical B-24 engine cowlings, a design borrowed from the PBY Catalina, did not have to be completely removed to work on the engines and ancillary equipment.

B-24D 42-40658 *Ole Sarge* 512th BS, 376th BG, 'belly-flopped on forced landing but still took it without injury to the crew'. *Ole Sarge* survived the Ploesti raid and was later shot down by a Bf 109G on 28 December 1943 southwest of Vincenza, Italy.

B-24D 41-23744 *Geronimo*, 328th BS, 93rd BG, crashed landed at Tafaraoui airfield, Algeria, after the nose wheel collapsed. The crew were uninjured. December 1942.

Consolidated B-24D 42-40654 *Kate Smith*, 345th BS, 98th BG, is overhauled by members of the 43rd Service Group at an airfield near Benghasi, Libya. Mechanical problems prevented the bomber from flying on the 1 August Ploesti mission.

Passionate debate about which was the 'better' bomber, the Boeing B-17 or Consolidated B-24, quickly began. Wartime Press Corp coverage of the more 'aesthetic' B-17 easily surpassed, some would say one-sidedly, that of the ungainly boxcar-like B-24. Each aircraft however differed in its design philosophy. A B-17 could reach a higher altitude and was easier to fly, while its counterpart was significantly faster, had a longer range, and carried a heavier payload. The B-24 could take even more punishment in combat due to its mid-mounted, high-lift 'Davis Wing', which reduced drag and bolstered structural integrity. In reality, however, no aircraft was truly superior to the other. Combat records also contradict the argument that the B-17 was the 'safer' aircraft. More B-24s were manufactured (a total of 18,482) than B-17s (12,731), yet the B-17 continued to soldier on postwar in large numbers while B-24s were rapidly taken out of service. In the end, both aircraft proved to be effective and versatile workhorses over enemy skies; the argument as to which bomber was the better continues.

Examining combat damage. The pilot's manual affirmed that it can 'take it and dish it out. The B-24's combat record is best told by those who have flown it through flak and swarming fighters, in mission after mission, and know first-hand what it can do… The B-24 has proved itself capable of delivering tremendous blows against the enemy over extremely long ranges, under unfavourable weather conditions and against heavy enemy opposition. If the gunners are properly trained, they can create havoc among enemy fighters. I have seen formations of B-24s penetrate heavily defended battle zones, completely destroy their target, fight off twice their number of enemy fighters and, through their manoeuvrability and firepower, destroy over 50% of all attacking fighters without loss to themselves… I have seen B-24s shot up by 88-mm anti-aircraft so badly it seemed impossible that the airplane could stay in the air. One pilot brought his B-24 back to base with half the rudder control completely shot away. We have had airplanes come back under almost unbelievable handicaps: with propellers shot off; with direct hits in gasoline cells by 20, 40 and 88-mm explosive shells, with the two lower engine supports knocked completely off; with both ailerons gone; after complete loss of rudder control; after loss of elevator control. Airplanes have returned with controls so badly damaged they were landed on autopilot.'

Chapter Six

Airfields and Airmen

Aerial view of the 301st BG airfield at Biskra, Algeria, December 1942. Notwithstanding the dust, Biskra was an effective bomber base with a massive runway that allowed three B-17s to take off abreast. The difficulties of operating in the desert were outlined in a 1943 US 9th Air Force publication: 'Sand's end-product, dust, was the common enemy of all combatants, revealing and hiding movement; filling slit trenches, coarsening food and thickening water. Borne on the wind, it blinded, choked and added to the general destruction of camp and equipment. The defeat of this enemy was the specific mission of the men in the shops and mechanics on the forward landing grounds… Two myths of the desert were exploded for the uninitiated. The night could be bitterly cold in December and January and the sand was only a coating, as discovered in digging in the brick-like soil underneath. The warmer British battledress and extra blankets had to be issued to officers and enlisted men alike. The sand storms began late in January. Clouds of choking, blinding dust whipped along by a high wind descended on the camp. Visibility was reduced to a few feet and it became difficult to find anything but the mess tent and little use to find it.'

Surveyor and graders prepare a new airfield. *Life* reported in December 1942 how some airports, in French Morocco for example, were 'little better than cow pastures'.

The same field three days later. Major General Eugene Reybold, the Chief of Army Engineers, could claim: 'A key to air power, the engineers now lay down in a few days airfields which a few years ago would have taken months. Engineers are still the Army pioneers.' Brigadier General S.C. Godfrey concurred: 'This story of the aviation engineers in Northwest Africa is the best evidence yet presented on rapid airdrome construction for a large air force in a new theatre. When I visited this theatre last December, the obstacles of mud, rainy weather, shortage of equipment and difficulty of supply were handicapping the untiring efforts of our engineer troops. But more men and especially more heavy equipment kept coming. As General Spaatz said in commending his aviation engineers, they "never failed to accomplish their objectives in time".'

Censored photo of a Clark CA-1 Airborne Bulldozer and a 'sheep's foot' roller.

A crusher breaks up rock for runway construction at Lourmel Airport, Oran, March 1943. When the Allies occupied North-West Africa, only five all-weather airfields were available. By the end of the Tunisian campaign, some 9,000 AAF aviation engineers had successfully constructed more than 100 additional airstrips.

The availability of heavy construction equipment in March 1943 enabled US aviation engineers to construct new airfields with improved speed and skill. Specifications dictated that forward airfields comprise one runway with loop taxiways and dispersed hardstands. No buildings were constructed, with munitions and fuel dumps located off existing roads. The machine on the right is a LeTourneau Super C Tournapull with Carryall Scraper.

Civilian labourers pile steel matting at an airfield at Valmy, Algeria, March 1943.

Engineers roll the runway at Lourmel airfield in Algeria. Used by the 12th Air Force, the airfield lies abandoned today.

Native labourers at work at the end Payne Field, Cairo, while a B-25 prepares to land. The airfield was transferred to Egypt after the war and renamed Farouk Airport. Today it is better known as Cairo International Airport.

'The comforts of home,' waxed a wartime writer, 'are left far behind at this command outpost somewhere in North Africa near the Tunisian front lines.' As the Allies quickly discovered during the winter of 1942-43, airfields in western Tunisia were prone to becoming unserviceable after heavy rainfall. *Air Force* magazine (January 1944) reported that 'it takes some time to become accustomed to distance in Africa. Somehow you get the idea that when you have a few days leave in Tunis you can hop to Cairo for a weekend. Then it dawns on you that the distance is about the same as from New York to San Francisco.'

The biggest enemy to man and machine in the desert was the sandstorm. Pictured are Technical Sergeant William G. Jordan (radio operator), 1st Lieutenant John E. McAtee (pilot) and Staff Sergeant Libert T. Hurt, radio operator and waist gunner, of B-24 41-237-24 *Doodle Bug*.

A booklet issued to US Army personnel described the climatic extremes that would be experienced in North Africa: 'A country of pronounced geographic contrasts. Along the land is almost as pleasant as Southern California, with hot, dry summers and consistently heavy rains in winter. The forested mountains of Morocco and Algeria have a heavy winter snowfall, and excellent skiing grounds. Temperatures in the higher altitudes of all the coastlands fall below freezing on winter nights. South of the mountains and plateaus the true desert begins. It is not a continuous sea of sand as is pictured in Hollywood movies about the French Foreign Legion. Some parts of the Sahara are great stretches of these picturesque dunes, but others are rim rock and gravel, and one may travel for days and see scarcely any sand. In places the horizon is perfectly flat while elsewhere the skyline may be broken by jagged hills or tablelands not unlike the mesas of New Mexico and Arizona. Most of the desert is too barren of vegetation to support cattle grazing, though camels and goats may subsist upon it. Rain falls but rarely, though then in such doses that bivouac commanders should take care not to make camp in a ravine or in the bottom of a desert valley. After sunset the desert cools off rapidly. The warmth of the winter sunshine is usually tempered by a steady wind, and the winter nights – especially in the highlands of the central Sahara or on the Libyan Plateau – are bitterly cold.

RAF pilots sheld themselves from flying sand. Note the Luftwaffe aircraft fuel tank trailer *Flugbetriebsstoff-Kesselwagen-Anhänger* *(Anh. B 2/1).*

American aviator Len Morgan recalled a 'solid yellow-brown wall of sand that blotted out the sun and reduced visibility to zero. We'd hunker down with towels wrapped around our heads, unable to see tentmates six feet away, and wait out the searing gale for hours, sometimes days… the air filled with grit and ochre dust with the consistency of flour. It got into your eyes, ears, nostrils, food, water, between book pages, everywhere. All activity ceased except that necessary to sustain life. It seeped into instruments, fuel tanks, pumps and radios. It pitted cylinders, reducing engine life to 200 hours, and peeled the paint off leading edges. Maintenance was a nightmare.' Technical Sergeant Arthur Maxfield wrote of a sandstorm at Gambut, Libya: 'A sand storm, the most violent I have ever seen, came up right at take off. Why it wasn't called off I'll never know, but it wasn't. Forty-eight planes were taxiing around in that storm with a visibility of fifteen feet, I think it was nine planes that got off, but for the rest it was murder. Some taxied into slit trenches, some taxied into each other, one hit a big rock and knocked six inches off its prop. The ground crews were frantically trying to lead the planes to the take off spot, but had to give up, for planes were going in all directions.'

Doughnuts and coffee are served by mobile Red Cross workers at an 'advanced US fighter base' while intelligence officers interrogate P-38 pilots post mission.

Aerial view of La Sénia airfield, Algeria. Capturing the former Armée de l'Air de Vichy airfield was one of the primary objectives of the Allied assault on Oran, 9 November 1942. La Sénia was subsequently used by the US 12th Air Force.

Damage to hangars and planes at Maison Blanche following a German air raid on the night of 20/21 November 1942. The raid destroyed B-17 41-24376, C-47 41-18369, and a P-38. Casualties were twenty personnel killed and a further twenty-eight wounded.

385th BG aircrew pose beside a captured German 60-cm *Flakscheinwerfer* (searchlight).

Ablaze with light, a 'death-dealing pattern' is seen over Algiers as Allied forces train anti-aircraft artillery and machine guns on German raiders. According to the wartime caption, the 'curtain of fire' brought down two German Ju 88 bombers. 26 March 1943.

Youks-les-Bains, Algeria. Engineers of the 814th Aviation Battalion at work with jack hammers on a bomb crater left by a 500-pound enemy bomb. According to the original caption, the men carry guns and wear helmets because of the frequent aerial attacks.

US Army engineers fill in a bomb crater beside an RAF Beaufighter.

A turret gun trainer used by the 376th BG is loaded with .50 calibre ammunition, Benghazi, Libya. Machine gun instruction was centred around the .50 calibre aircraft model, which was standard on US bombers. Students were required to strip and reassemble the gun blindfolded. By 1944 the standard gunnery course consisted of six weeks of equipment familiarisation and ground firing, in addition to air, military and physical training.

African-American troops served as air base security on some North Africa airfields. Pictured here is a unit from a security battalion running through an alert with their M-3 Gun Motor Carriage, a tank destroyer armed with a 75-mm gun.

Sheet-metal workers patched damaged skin. The thickness of B-17 skin, for example, varied from .025 to .051 gauge, depending on the load it was required to carry. Although the Fortress was a rugged aircraft, a man could easily pierce the thin metal skin with a screwdriver. Strength within the bomber came from its clever design and the use of interlocking structural members.

Civilian workers remove nicks and smooth damaged blades in this Algerian propeller shop.

Technical Sergeant J.M. Phillips, of the 346th Service Squadron, 310th BG, sands down a Plexiglass patch in a turret pierced by shrapnel. Berteaux, March 1943.

Newly arrived US aircrew in North Africa learnt many useful and lifesaving tips from the British such as spacing tents by 50 paces and aircraft by 250 paces. Slit trenches were dug for protection against strafing and bombing.

Fighting the blaze from a collision between two C-47 transports. Len Morgan, who flew with the USAAF in Africa and the Middle East, wrote how the 'jolting' North African temperatures had a dramatic effect on transport flight operations. The 'desert pink' C-47s, 2,500 pounds heavier at take-off than the stateside DC-3 maximum, would roll an alarming distance to become airborne. 'They struggled for altitude at 100 feet a minute with head temps in the red. Under extreme conditions, high-performance types were launched at dawn or not at all.'

26 January 1943. Lieutenant General Henry 'Hap' Arnold – widely considered as the general who established the US Air Force – addresses airmen at a US air base in the Western Desert. Arnold was opposed to Operation Torch, the invasion of North Africa, believing that it was a distraction from the task of bombing Germany.

B-25 crews receive last-minute instructions from an intelligence officer, Western Desert, Egypt.

Benghazi, Libya. Colonel Keith K. Compton, commanding officer of the 376th BG, 9th Air Force (left), and Major N.C. Arnold, group operations officer, brief pilots before the 13 August 1943 bombing raid on the Messerschmitt aircraft factory at Wiener Neustadt, Austria, less than two weeks after the fateful Ploesti raid. The Wiener Neustadt plant was the main Messerschmitt factory, producing 49 per cent of Germany's Bf 109 fighters. Pictured standing is Lieutenant Norman C. Appold, pilot of B-24 42-40657 *G.I. Ginnie*.

Compton instructs B-24 aircrew about Wiener Neustadt raid in the outdoor briefing theatre. Originally scheduled for 7 August, the mission was cancelled because of bad weather. Note: there will be no movie tonight!

Maison Blanch, Algeria, October 1943. Men of the 36th Air Depot Group check B-17 engines on a test block prior to installation. Before 1939, the basic aircraft mechanics course, covering first and second echelon maintenance, was taught over a thirty-eight week period. To accelerate training, the length of the course was progressively shortened and by July 1943 it had been more than halved to 112 days. Basic training included preliminary instruction in the use of tools, followed by the practical study of aircraft structures, operating systems, instruments, engines, and propellers. Once a student was familiar with an aircraft, attention was given to engine changes, pre-flight and daily inspections as well as more thorough periodic inspections. About one week of maintenance and testing under simulated field conditions was undertaken towards the end of the course.

A Federal Type C-2 wrecker hauls a spare bomber engine to a supply depot at La Sénia airfield, Algeria. June 1943.

Overhauling a B-24 Pratt & Whitney Twin Wasp R-1830-43 fourteen-cylinder, two row, radial engine. Manufacturer instructions specified that when 'an engine is new or has just been overhauled, it should be given a thorough check no later than thirty hours after it has been installed in the airplane.' A periodic inspection schedule contained four intervals: 'A' fifty-hour inspection, a 'B' 100 hour, 'C' 200 hour and 'D', the midpoint between overhauls. Maintenance guidelines specified that when it is known that a bomber will be idle for more than one day, but not more than seven days, the engine should be operated every second day at 1,000 rpm for fifteen minutes or until the oil temperature reaches 65°C (149°F).

Native workers load 500-pound aerial bombs aboard an ordnance truck at an Air Service depot. An American soldier operates the 2-ton M3 crane tractor (built by International Harvester) while another GI inspects the bomb fuse at lower left. Each bomb was painted in dull olive drab with a 25 mm yellow band at the nose and a 42 mm yellow band 140 mm from the end. There were two types of explosive fillings—TNT, or a 50/50 Amatol and TNT mix. The weight of the filling was 262 pounds; each bomb weighed 531 pounds. The square box-type tail fin assemblies are yet to be attached. The circular shipping bands are channelled to fit over the suspension lugs around the circumference of the bomb. They protect the lugs and allow the bombs to be rolled along a hard surface.

Squadron Headquarters. Major Bernard Muldoon and pilots of the 49th FS, 14th FG, synchronise their watches.

Briefing crews before a mission, 1943. A diagnosis of 'flying fatigue' was given to certain aircrew whose efficiency had begun to deteriorate after a prolonged period in combat. Nervous disorders would eventually account for most flying casualties in the Twelfth Air Force from November 1943 to May 1944.

Informal discussion, albeit posed for the camera, after an operation. The US Air Force concluded after the war that 'The average aircrewman may have been handy with dice or cards, but he never understood statistics. The way he interpreted it, the rising curve for the percentage of the group killed and missing in action spelled a steady decrease in his personal chance of survival. He never understood the significance of the broken line showing the risk rate per mission, which became increasingly more favorable as the 25-mission tour progressed. The net result was that the old soldier's protection against anxiety, the delusion that "nothing can happen to me," was replaced by the morale-destroying fixation that "something disastrous must happen to me." There was nothing definite that the flight surgeon could do about this, except talk to the ones that had it worst, prescribe phenobarbital and Benzedrine, arrange for a rest leave, and hope for the best.'

Decoration ceremony, Libya.

Major General James H. Doolittle pins the Distinguished Flying Cross (DFC) on Major Wade C. Walles, commanding officer of the 48th FS. February 1943.

Major James G. Curl was awarded the British DSO for 'courage, determination and devotion to duty' in leading the history-making raid at Cape Bon, Tunisia. Also known as the 'Palm Sunday Massacre', the US 57th FG shot down seventy-five enemy aircraft. In the course of his service career, Curl also received the Silver Star, Air Medal, American Campaign Medal and the WWII Victory Medal. Killed on 19 March 1945, Curl is buried at Lorraine American Cemetery, St. Avold, France.

Sergeant Charles A Lawson is awarded the Air Medal by Brigadier General Patrick Timberlake, 9th AF. The Air Medal was authorized by President Roosevelt by Executive Order 9158, dated 11 May 1942 for 'any person who, while serving in any capacity in the Army, Navy, Marine Corps or Coast Guard of the United States subsequent to September 8, 1939, distinguishes, or has distinguished, himself by meritorious achievement while participating in an aerial flight.'

Rewarded for gallantry. 1st Lieutenant Jackson B. Clayton (co-pilot) proudly displays a Silver Star presented to him on 11 November 1942 by Lieutenant General Frank M. Andrews, Commanding General of US Air Forces in the Middle East. Clayton's award recognised his initiative to shut down an engine after a fuel pump malfunction thirty minutes from the target, the port of Tobruk. This allowed the pilot to continue individually and not hinder the bombing airspeed of a formation of B-24s. The pilot completed his mission in the face of heavy anti-aircraft fire, which holed his plane in numerous places. An additional problem was a frozen hydraulic system, which caused a temporary fire and rendered the tail turret inoperable.

General Brereton presents 2nd Lieutenant Dale R. Deniston with the DFC.

Lieutenant Colonel Elliott Roosevelt displays his newly awarded DFC, below the Silver Wings, on his winter service dress uniform. He wears the standard officers' peaked cap.

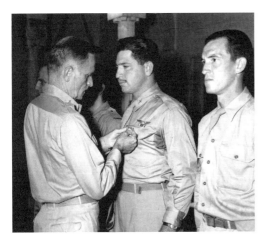

Lt. Gen. Carl A. Spaatz presents an award to Lt. Webb of 90th Photographic Wing (Reconnaissance).

General Spaatz, Commander of the Northwest African Air Forces, receives the Legion of Merit Medal from Allied Commander in Chief General Dwight D. Eisenhower.

General Andrews presents the Silver Star to 2nd Lieutenant Donald M. Wilder.

Twelfth Air Force camp, Algiers.

Desert life – canvas and slit trenches.

An air raid siren sounds.

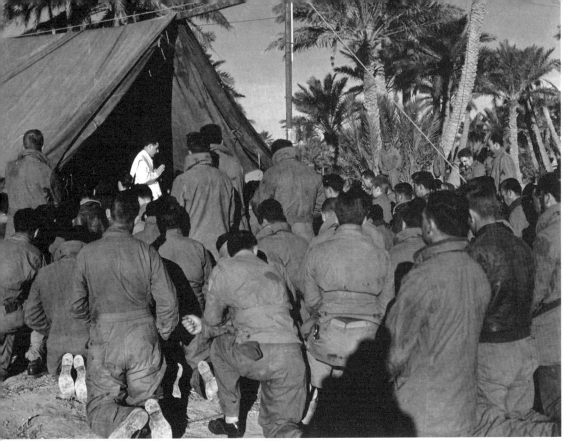

Outdoor Catholic mass, Algeria. Some 9,000 US Army chaplains served in the field during the war.

'Clean up time for these men somewhere in the Western Desert, Egypt'.

Life (12 April 1943) detailed the rudimentary desert living conditions: 'When the first British and American fliers arrived in Algeria and Tunisia, they were forced to sleep on the ground under their planes. The weather was cold and the barren fields muddy. Today things are better, but living conditions are still crude. The men have shovelled for dugouts into streambeds and the sides of gullies. Old Roman ruins are frequently used as mess halls. Stoves are built of ammunition trays, fireplaces of gasoline cans, faucets of hydraulic control valves. Straw matting bought from Arabs serves as flooring, and abandoned wing jacks often hold up dugout roofs. The most ingenious men, of course, have the most comfortable dugouts.'

These men wear the standard fatigue 'baseball' cap.

Algiers. Rugged up against the desert cold and ready for chow. *Air Force* magazine (January & February 1943) explained the weather in North Africa as divided into two periods: 'The hot dry period from June to September, and the dust/rain-storm period from September to May… Spring and fall are the best operational seasons.' And it's cold. 'Algeria is in the same latitude as North Carolina but without the benefit of the Gulf Stream. If you're moving into the area take winter uniforms.'

Air Force, October 1943, reported on this 'Base Oasis in North Africa', a recreation centre complete with the tail from a fallen Messerschmitt Bf 110.

'Airmen get fed up at times with all work and no play. And there are comparatively few opportunities for recreation in the field in North Africa. But one B-26 squadron worked out a solution by building a "community" centre out of odds and ends of available scrap material. It's not finished as the average club in the States, but it's a howling success just the same… Wood for the building, which came mostly from packing boxes for fragmentation bombs, was collected after an unrelenting search. Heavy beams and posts served originally as crates for heavy equipment. Tents and tent flies made a neat waterproof roof. The structure is portable and the squadron fondly hopes to pack it along if and when it moves to another location. The lumber alone makes the building precious in the land of few trees.'

Members of the Earthquakers BG relax between missions with a game of volleyball.

Instruments reclaimed from derelict aircraft are tagged for reuse.

Tangled aircraft wreckage at Telergma, Algeria, where damaged aircraft beyond repair are brought for salvage. Many pilots and aircrew, according to *Air Force* (September 1943), salvaged armour plate from wrecked planes, which they would use for additional protection. This makeshift protection apparently stopped many fragments that could have resulted in injury.

Oxygen tanks,
wheels and tyres are
recovered and reused.

The burnt-out remains of a C-47 are inspected at Algiers. Known by US pilots as the Skytrain, the C-47 was the most widely used transport aircraft of the war. It was cited by General Eisenhower as one of the four weapons that contributed most to ending the war, the others being the Jeep, Bazooka and Atomic bomb.

C-47 wreckage is examined at Biskra following a German air attack on 15 January 1943. Of interest is the pre-war US insignia on the fuselage featuring a red circle on a white star. The red element was unofficially removed in December 1941 and officially withdrawn in May 1942 to prevent any confusion with Imperial Japanese insignia

Evacuation of wounded, Algieria. No army hospitals were located east of Algiers until after March 1943 when an evacuation hospital was established in Constantine. Many of the Army Air Force medical personnel had little or no specialised training in combat or aviation medicine.

Note the line-up of waiting Dodge WC 54 4x4 ambulances, the main US Army ambulance from 1942 to 1945. A total of 26,002 were produced.

Evacuation of wounded aboard Douglas C-47s 41-19473 (above) and C-47 41-18685 (below). The twin-engined transport functioned as an aeromedical workhorse in North Africa.

Aerial evacuation of wounded became critical in mid-January 1943 when US troops entered southern Tunisia. With few available hospitals, railways or roads, the trip by road in an ambulance to Constantine took up to twenty-four hours while aerial evacuation took only sixty to ninety minutes to hospitals in Algiers and Oran. By 29 May 1943 the Twelfth Air Force had carried some 15,000 patients by air from Tunisia with only one mid-flight fatality. An evacuation kit aboard most C-47 tranports contained blood plasma, first-aid medicine, oxygen, morphine, portable heaters, and bandages to control haemorrhaging. Patients for aerial evacuation were selected by flight surgeons and usually accompanied by medical technicians and flight nurses, many of whom flew as air stewardesses before the war. Surgeons would sometimes accompany critically ill patients. Each C-47 would usually carry eighteen to twenty-four litter patients.

Bodies of Air Force dead are loaded onto a truck for transportation to the Pax Cemetery at Casablanca for reburial.

Hazards after the battle. Flying Officer Harry Rowe and Staff Sergeant Robert F. Burchard, both of the 37th Squadron, 316th Troop Carrier Group, were killed when a German mortar bomb they were examining exploded on 19 February 1943. Chaplain T.S. Cordill, Jr places a cross on each grave in the Tobruk Cemetery. Over and above regular ordnance littering a battlefield, retreating Axis forces adopted variations to their usual methods of laying mines and preparing booby traps to slow the Allied advance. US engineers had to learn the tricks that Germans used to slow down clearance teams. Mines could be booby-trapped or laid up to a metre deep. Vehicles would pass safely over the mine until a rut developed deep enough to explode the mine. Scattered scrap metal was also used to fool Allied mine detectors. At the conclusion of the North African Campaign, the US 9th Infantry Division concluded that the 'failure to recognise the fact that the enemy is a master in the art of mining and booby-trapping will cost lives.'

Funeral service near *La Sénia* Airfield, Algeria, for 1st Lieutenant Wesley M. Pringle Jr, who died as a non-battle (DNB) casualty on 28 May 1943. Pringle enlisted on 23 November 1940 at Fort Bragg, North Carolina, Army Serial Number 14034702. Recipient of the Air Medal and 2 Oak Leaf Clusters, he is buried at the North American Cemetery, Carthage, Tunisia.

General Spaatz places a wreath on the grave of an unknown US soldier.

White crosses mark the graves of American soldiers in a military cemetery somewhere in North Africa, November 1943.

A bent propeller blade marks the field grave of 1st Lieutenant Ober N. Leatherman, 86th FS, 79th FG. Leatherman was shot down in his P-40 Kittyhawk by enemy ground fire during the Battle of Wadi Akarit on 6 April 1943. Born on 8 July 1913, Leatherman is buried at Arlington National Cemetery.

Appendix I

USAAF Casualties in European, North African, and Mediterranean Theatres of Operation, 1942–1946 (Derived from Department of the Army, "Army Battle Casualties and Nonbattle Deaths in World War II – Final Report" [Washington, DC: Dept of Army, GPO, 1 June 1953], pp.84–88)

Killed in Action	
ETO	23,805
North Africa and MTO	9,997
Total KIA	33,802
Wounded and Injured in Action (Died of wounds)	.
ETO	9,299 (510)
NATO and MTO	4,428 (276)
Total wounded	13,727 (786)
Captured and Interned (POWs dying in captivity)	
ETO[a]	26,064 (148)
NATO and MTO	7,350 (54)
Total captured	33,414 (202)
Missing in Action (returned to duty)	
ETO	2,853 (2,316)
North Africa and MTO	3,642 (3,125)
Total MIA	6,495 (5,441)
Total Casualties (ETO)	62,021
Total Casualties (North Africa) and MTO	25,417
Total AAF (All theaters) KIA	44,785
Total AAF (All theaters) Wounded or Injured in Action (Died in Captivity)	18,364 (1,004)
Total AAF (All theaters) Captured and Interned (Died in Captivity)	41,057 (2,783)
Total AAF (All theaters) MIA (returned to duty)	11,176 (7,556)
Total AAF (All theaters) Casualties	115,382
Total AAF Aircraft Accident Deaths (7 December 1941– 31 Dec 1946)	25,844

[a]This figure apparently includes all AAF prisoners recovered from POW camps in Germany. It would, therefore, count a great many American aircrews captured by the Germans in the Mediterranean (belonging to the Ninth, Twelfth, and Fifteenth Air Forces) and thence transferred to Germany.